Contents

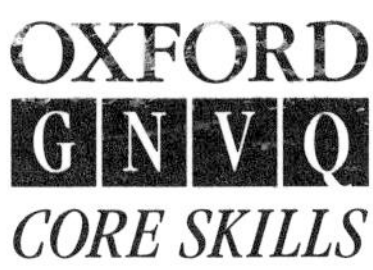

Communication

JAMES SIMMS

Oxford University Press 1995

Oxford University Press, Walton Street, Oxford OX2 6DP

Oxford New York
Athens Auckland Bangkok Bombay
Calcutta Cape Town Dar es Salaam Delhi
Florence Hong Kong Istanbul Karachi
Kuala Lumpur Madras Madrid Melbourne
Mexico City Nairobi Paris Singapore
Taipei Tokyo Toronto

and associated companies in
Berlin Ibadan

Oxford is a trademark of Oxford University Press

First published 1995

A CIP catalogue record for this book is available from the British Library.

ISBN 0 19 831291 1 (non net edition)
ISBN 0 19 831285 7 (net edition)

Typeset and designed by Oxprint Ltd

Printed and bound in Great Britain

Introduction to core skills: communication

What are communication skills?

Communication skills are the skills we use in understanding and presenting information and ideas through spoken and written language. The ability to use these skills well is central to education and training and in the work place.

GNVQ builds on the communication skills you already have from your study of English language and seeks to improve these skills and help you progress to a higher level of ability. You will also find GNVQ skills relate directly to what is expected in real situations and not just in academic study.

How communication skills are related to GNVQ

Whatever GNVQ you are taking and at whatever level, you are required to develop your communication skills. The skills are divided into four themes:

- taking part in discussions
- preparing written materials
- using images to illustrate points made in writing and in discussions
- reading and responding to written material and images

Progress in each of these themes is measured in levels 1 to 5, beginning with basic skills and progressing to the most advanced and sophisticated. The levels relate to the three main levels of GNVQ attainment which are: Foundation – minimum level 1; Intermediate – minimum level 2; Advanced – minimum level 3. As you progress up the levels you are required to apply your skills to an increasing range of situations, audience and materials.

It is easy to know what level you have reached simply by reading the descriptions attached to each. These descriptions are called the *performance criteria* and it is important to become familiar with these in order to know how far you have progressed.

The performance criteria

The performance criteria for each of the themes and each level look like this:

Level 1

1.1 Take part in discussions with known individuals on routine matters.

1.2 Prepare written materials in pre-set formats.

1.3 Use images to illustrate points made in writing and in discussions with known individuals on routine matters.

1.4 Read and respond to written material and images in pre-set formats.

Level 2

2.1 Take part in discussions with a range of people on routine matters.
2.2 Prepare written material on routine matters.
2.3 Use images to illustrate points made in writing and in discussions with a range of people on routine matters.
2.4 Read and respond to written material and images on routine matters.

Level 3

3.1 Take part in discussions with a range of people on a range of matters.
3.2 Prepare written material on a range of matters.
3.3 Use images to illustrate points made in writing and in discussions with a range of people on a range of matters.
3.4 Read and respond to written material and images on a range of matters.

Level 4

4.1 Take part in, and evaluate the effectiveness of, discussions with a range of people on a range of matters.
4.2 Prepare, and evaluate the effectiveness of, own written material on a range of matters.
4.3 Use and evaluate the effectiveness of own use of images to illustrate points made in writing and in discussions with a range of people on a range of matters.
4.4 Read and respond to written material and images, recognising the factors which influence own interpretation.

Level 5

5.1 Lead, and evaluate the effectiveness of, discussions with a range of people on a range of matters.
5.2 Prepare, and evaluate the effectiveness of, own and others' written material on a range of matters.
5.3 Use and evaluate the effectiveness of own and others' use of images to illustrate points made in writing and in discussions with a range of people on a range of matters.
5.4 Read and respond to written material and images, recognising the factors which influence own and others' interpretation.

Please note
You are not expected to remember the full details of the performance criteria. However, it is important to refer back to them to see what progress you have made and to make sure you are meeting the course requirements.

How communication skills are learnt, demonstrated and tested in GNVQ

Communication skills are part of the core skills common to all GNVQs. You will be learning and using the skills throughout your course and you can expect to find them integrated into the main subject of your GNVQ study. You can also be credited for achievement in communication skills while in situations and with people beyond college; for example, on work experience, in part-time work, or on a residential field study.

For example, suppose you are taking a GNVQ in Health and Social Care. Unit 3 of this course deals with Health Emergencies and for one element of this students are asked to show evidence that they can write a report of methods for stopping contamination. This is just one example of communication skills at work in the main area of study.

Remember – communication skills are an integral part of all your GNVQ studies.

A question of evidence

As you progress through your GNVQ you will be asked to perform a broad range of tasks and activities, most of which will contain elements of communication skills. Because there is no end-of-course examination in the core skills, the responsibility is on you to show evidence of what you have achieved and how you managed this.

This evidence is collected in your portfolio of coursework. The contents of your portfolio can include written, audio and video evidence from:

- projects
- assignments
- activities

Remember – you always need to be on the look out for good examples of coursework to use as evidence in your portfolio.

How this book will help

The units in this book will help you:

- get to know the essential skills
- cover the range of situations, materials and audiences required for GNVQ
- to focus on particular skills
- get to know the quality of work expected

There are also a number of exercises throughout the book which enable you to produce the kind of evidence that is considered valuable in a coursework portfolio. The book follows the four main themes of communication skills and is structured in this way:

- the theme – e.g. taking part in discussion
- what you need to know about that theme – all about subject, situation, audience etc.
- information about the skills related to that theme and how to evaluate the skills – using the telephone, body language, working in a group etc.
- skills in practice – a number of exercises designed to give you lots of practice with all the skills related to the theme. These exercises also enable you to produce evidence for your portfolio.

1

Oral skills

Taking part with others in a discussion on a range of matters

Speaking is the way in which most people communicate. How you speak and what you say depends on:

- who you are speaking to
- for what reason
- the situation in which it takes place

For most people speaking is easy when:

- they are relaxed with their audience (friends or family)
- the subject is what they want to talk about (sport/music)
- the situation suits them (their home or the pub)

Answer these questions:

- Who do you feel most comfortable with when you are having a discussion?
- What subject do you enjoy talking about with others?
- Where or in what situation do you feel relaxed and able to talk freely?

Unfortunately it isn't always possible to be in control of the factors that make speaking easy. In your college and school life, as well as in the world of work beyond education, you will be expected to speak to a range of people, on a range of subjects, in many different situations. Getting to know the oral skills needed for clear and effective speaking to people known and unknown to you is an important part of your GNVQ.

How this chapter will help you

As part of your GNVQ core skills communication, you need to develop effective oral skills for speaking and listening generally and taking part in discussions in particular. In this chapter you will get to know about:

- the range of oral skills you are expected to use
- the purpose of your talk
- the importance of tone and manner
- listening to and including others in your discussion

The range of oral skills you are expected to use in GNVQ

- For Foundation, Intermediate and Advanced levels you are expected to be able to:
  - talk with people you know face to face
  - talk about your day-to-day work

- For Intermediate and Advanced Levels you are **also** expected to:
  - talk with people on the telephone
  - talk with people you do not know about your subject
- For Advanced Level you are **also** expected to:
  - talk with people you do not know and who do not know your subject
  - talk about non-routine, complicated subjects

What about the quality of your speaking and listening (or what is called the *performance criteria*)? For all Levels (Foundation, Intermediate and Advanced) your speaking and listening needs to:

- be clear and to the point
- be of a suitable manner and tone for the people you are talking to
- show that you listen carefully to others
- show that you can ask questions to check you understand what has been said

- For Advanced Level you are **also** expected to show you can:
  - encourage others to join in discussion

Understanding the purpose

Like written work, all discussion has a purpose or reason. Here are some:

- to exchange information
- to arrive at a conclusion
- to make a decision
- to discuss an issue
- to consider the pros and cons of an idea

Exercise 1 (a)

E

Can you guess what the likely purpose is behind these discussions? Use one of the five categories above.

Between	Subject	Purpose
A doctor and her patient	Test results	
A tutor and his student	Assessment of main subject assignment	
Mechanic and car owner	MOT test	
A teacher and parent	School report	
Bank manager and account holder	Account statement	
Manager and employee	Wage increase	

Exercise 1 (b)

Make a list of the people you spend most of your week talking to, in social as well as work situations. Next to each write down the usual subject of discussion. Note the purpose beside each (see grid above). You should now be able to answer the following question.

- What is the main purpose for your discussion in an average week?

Understanding the purpose behind your discussion helps you to keep to the point in your discussion. For example: John's task was to discuss with a small group of fellow students how he could use computer graphics in his next science assignment. After ten minutes the latest computer game had become the subject of the discussion.

How and why do you think this discussion went wrong?

Tips for keeping to the point in discussion

(a) Before discussion begins it is useful to state and agree the purpose with the others taking part.

'So the reason why we are discussing this assignment is to agree on a suitable title.'

(b) Sum up regularly during the discussion how far you have got with the purpose.

'At this stage it looks like we have agreed on the first part of the title.'

(c) Remind anyone who begins to drift off the subject, about the purpose of the discussion. This needs to be done gently. A reminder in the form of a question is often a good method.

'That's an interesting point, but do you feel it's important to the main purpose of our discussion?'

(d) In a group which often work together, it is sometimes a good idea to elect one person in rotation to alert the others when the discussion begins to drift.

Understanding the subject

At Foundation and Intermediate Levels you are expected to take part in discussion on subjects which are routine, e.g.:

- responding to day-to-day enquiries
- discussing day-to-day matters or business

At Advanced Level you are **also** expected to be able to take part in discussion on subjects which are non-routine, e.g.:

- dealing with unfamiliar situations or matters
- discussing complex issues or dealing with sensitive issues

Exercise 1 (c)

When the subject is familiar, you will probably know the vocabulary related to that subject. Your knowledge of the subject should give you confidence and help you make points in discussion.

Which of these subjects are familiar to you?

◆ Football ◆ Golf ◆ Car maintenance ◆ Tennis ◆ Rave music ◆ Cats ◆ Mountain climbing ◆ Hospitals ◆ Personal computers ◆ Sailing ◆ The top twenty ◆ Mountain bikes ◆ Hair dressing ◆ Health food ◆ Rail travel ◆ Stamps ◆ Cooking ◆ The National Lottery ◆ Fishing ◆ School ◆ Child care ◆ Philosophy ◆ Fashion ◆ Cosmetics ◆ Wind surfing

Select any two subjects from the above and make spider diagrams of ideas and issues relating to the subjects. For example:

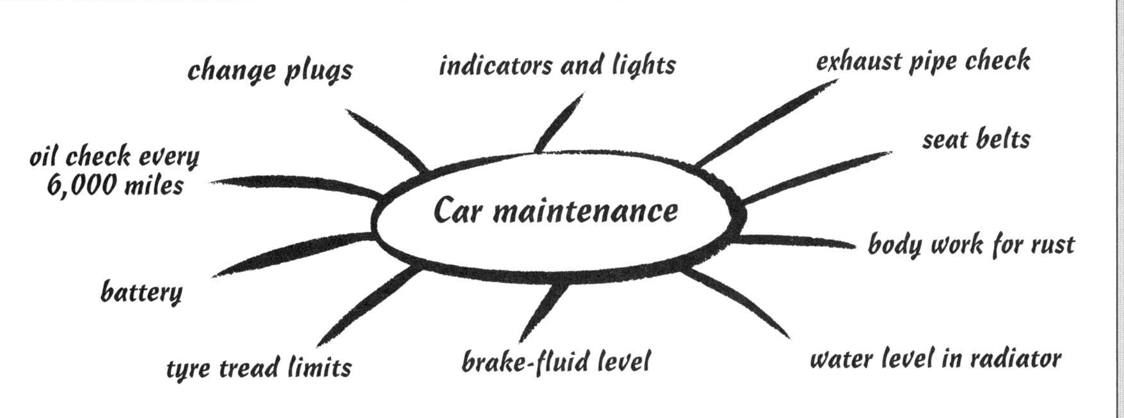

Exercise 1 (d)

Read the following extracts and decide which represent a subject that would generate a lively group discussion in your class. Can you explain why?

Extract A

'Smokers should be completely segregated in offices, factories, pubs and restaurants, says a new government report.'

Top scientists warn that drastic action is needed because non-smokers may face a 30% higher risk of lung cancer simply by breathing in other people's smoke. They believe passive smoking may be responsible for several hundred out of the current annual total of 40,000 lung cancer deaths in the UK. Smoking by parents may also increase the frequency and severity of childhood respiratory illnesses.

Extract B

'If you heard of a mergers and acquisitions team that had completed more than 500 deals worth £7.7 billion over the last decade without charging fees, would you hire them, fire them or float them on the stock exchange?

The answer is none of the above. ICI's chairman Sir Denys Henderson might just offer his M&A team a glass of Chablis on their tenth anniversary next month. While many of their deals barely register on the M&A Richter scale, the big ones have been Big. In 1984, Sir John Harvey-Jones, former trouble-shooting boss of ICI, ruled that the Company was unable to generate enough growth organically. It had to hit the acquisition trail.'

Extract C

'The steady growth in vegetarianism is being given a sudden boost with a campaign which is proving highly successful in schools. While more adults are turning to vegetarian diets for health reasons, their offspring are far more likely to be converted on the grounds of cruelty to animals.

Scream!, the School Campaign for Reaction Against Meat, is the new youth pressure group of the Vegetarian Society, which is sending information packs on the real horrors of factory farming and abuse of animals into schools, and offering to give talks and show a video on the subject. Emotive stuff.'

Remember, for good communication to take place in discussion it is important to:

- know if the subject is routine or non-routine to the speakers and listeners
- be sensitive and make allowances for others who may not know much about the subject
- always try to make the others feel valued for what they have to say
- get to know as much as possible about the subject to help your own contribution

E ***Exercise 1 (e)***

Can you explain the difference between routine and non-routine subjects?

Can you explain the difference between familiar and unfamiliar?

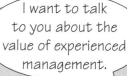

I want to talk to you about the value of experienced management.

The situation

The situation, or the context in which a discussion takes place, can be either formal or informal. It can vary from the happy, celebratory atmosphere of a wedding reception, to the more serious atmosphere of a business meeting. Depending on the context, the ways in which discussion takes place are likely to be very different.

Exercise 1 (f)

E

Match situations (a) to (g) below with one of these categories:

- light-hearted and lively
- businesslike
- whispering
- shouting

(a) Twenty-first birthday party
(b) Crowded football stadium
(c) Interview with potential employer
(d) Church or religious service
(e) Library
(f) School or college classroom
(g) House of Commons

Taking part in a discussion

Whatever the subject, taking part in a discussion involves a balance of speaking and listening skills. However, it is not always easy to get the balance right. Some people:

- don't say enough
- say too much
- don't listen to others

Do any of these describe your own performance in a discussion, or do you get the balance right most of the time?

Exercise 1 (g)

E

Would you consider the following statements true or false?

A good contribution to a discussion means:

- answering questions using Yes and No
- talking a lot
- pleasing others with what you say
- talking directly about the subject
- repeating the same point until you feel everyone has heard it
- talking over the top of others
- using a range of body language (e.g. nods and smiles etc.) to support others
- remaining silent until asked for your view
- asking questions
- bringing others into the discussion
- not asking questions
- disagreeing politely
- listening carefully to others

Discuss these points with a friend or small group. Try to add to the list of points you feel make a good contribution. Explain your choice to others. What action would you suggest to make sure everyone uses these oral skills in discussion?

The skills

This section looks at some of the skills linked to good performance in discussion.

Tone

Using the right tone is a valuable and necessary skill for good communication.

One of your main tasks when talking with others or to an audience is to get them to listen. The tone and manner in which you speak play a major part in this. The wrong tone can distract from what you are saying.

For example:
Suppose you were asked to take part in a group discussion on the subject of animal rights. The discussion may be with one of the following three groups:

- your friends and peers
- your tutors and teachers
- your parents and/or their friends

In what way would your tone and manner of speaking differ with each group? Can you explain why?

Here are some common mistakes to look out for:

- using pompous expressions in order to sound important
- using more words than are needed
- using worn-out cliches and gobbledygook (fancy words that don't make sense)
- trying to make others feel inferior by the volume and superior tone of your speech
- using words the audience will not understand
- believing the audience understands everything
- believing the audience understands very little

Tone is an aspect of oral performance that is often difficult to describe, but easily felt when it is wrong or inappropriate. For example, the word *yes* can be said in a sharp angry tone which suggests the speaker actually means *no*.

Here are some more examples. Try saying these words and phrases in a tone that contradicts their literal meaning:

- I'm really happy
- That sounds interesting
- I'm not nervous
- Delicious
- No
- The meal was fabulous
- Exciting
- Excuse me
- I'm not angry

Body language matters

Do you find the following statements convincing?

'He said he wasn't afraid, but I could tell from the look on his face that he really was.'

'She said she really enjoyed the concert, but everybody who saw her there said she looked totally bored.'

'I could tell by his eyes, he just wasn't interested.'

Body language, or non verbal communication, refers to the unspoken messages and signals we convey with our body.

Whatever our beliefs or opinions, our emotions are usually revealed in:

- how we stand or sit
- our facial expression
- hand gestures
- eye contact or lack of eye contact
- our general movements

Exercise 1 (h)

E

Study the figures in (a) to (g) on the next two pages. Given the following situations, what can you say about the body language of the various figures? What messages and signals are they sending?

(a) Applicants for a job
(b) Interviewers
(c) Team members in a group discussion
(d) Group discussion
(e) Group discussion
(f) Social gathering (guests at a party)
(g) Job interview with employer, applicant and observer

Make a list of all your points for each figure. Compare your notes with a friend.

Exercise 1 (i)

E

You are the manager of a busy restaurant. What guidelines would you produce as a reminder to your new staff on how to speak to your customers? Make a list of five points you believe are important for your staff to know:

- about the reasons why people come to your restaurant
- about the fact that not all your customers understand English very well
- about their tone of voice and body language
- about answering questions about the menu

Some of your regular customers are:

- large groups of lively students
- middle aged and senior citizens
- tourists who speak very little English
- a group of local hotel managers

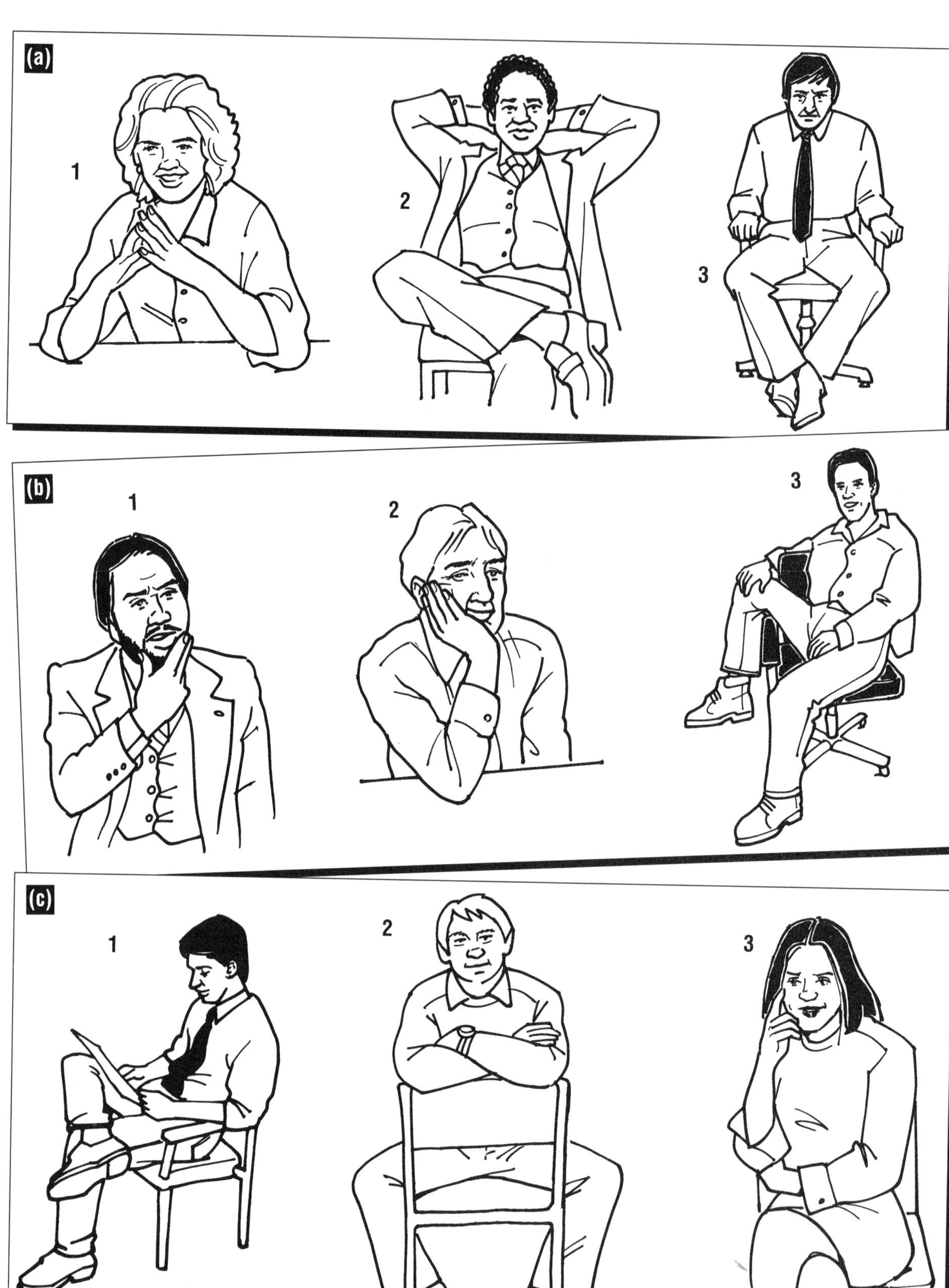
(a)
1
2
3
(b)
1
2
3
(c)
1
2
3

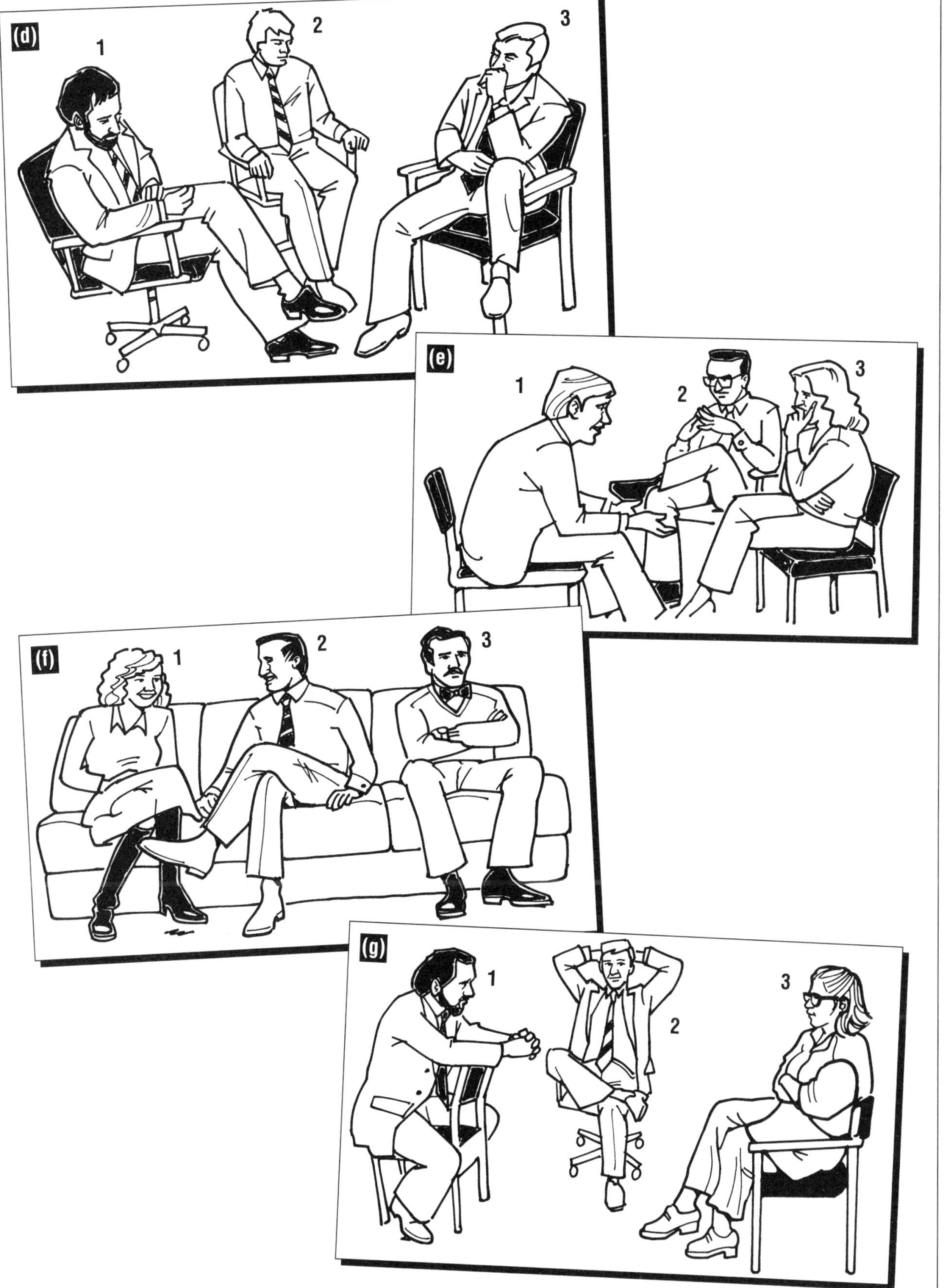
(d)
1
2
3
(e)
1
2
3
(f)
1
2
3
(g)
1
2
3

Some higher level skills

Using the telephone

The first thing to remember when you are using the phone is that you will not be seen by your listener. This means:

- you need to make it clear who you are and/or who you represent as soon as you begin
- the normal face language of smiles, frowns, surprise, sadness, has to be conveyed through your voice, mostly by tone
- body language also cannot be seen; without these normal aids the words you use therefore need to be precise and direct

Expecting the unexpected

Always prepare before you make a phone call. This means:

- know why you are calling and what you want to say
- have a pen and note paper ready for information you may receive during the call
- have ready any text or information – reference number, letters, memos, dates, times, calender, diary – you think might help with certain subjects or questions likely to arise
- if you happen to be calling from a pay phone, make sure you have enough coins for the call time you anticipate

Your telephone technique

(a) First give your name, who you wish to speak to and the reason why you are calling.

'Hello, this is Pauline Stone speaking. I would like to speak to Mr Rogers about a delivery of shoes that haven't arrived.'

(b) If you have lots of information or important dates to give, ask the listener if they have a pen and paper ready. If they haven't, give them a chance to get these before you continue with the call.

'Have you got a pen and paper ready? I think you'll need to jot this down.'

or

'Have you got your diary to hand? I need to confirm some dates with you for our meetings next month.'

(c) Important information or dates need to be repeated at the end of the call.

(d) Make sure you are talking to the right person before you begin to explain your subject in detail.

(e) Always speak slowly and clearly.

(f) If your recipient asks you to repeat what you've said, always do so willingly because:

- they may be hard of hearing
- while you may be able to hear them perfectly, this does not mean they can hear you with the same clarity

(g) Learn to be sympathetic and patient.

(h) If you are speaking on behalf of a business or organisation, explain what your role is.

'Good morning. This is Peter Wright , technical support engineer for Mori Computers. I understand you have a problem.'

Receiving calls

(a) Depending on the circumstances, when you receive a call give:

- your number
- the name of the company
- your name

(b) If you don't hear a name or any piece of information properly, ask the caller to repeat it. If they are still talking too quickly or it's a bad line, ask them to spell it out. If you want to be sure, read the information back to the caller and ask them to confirm that it is correct.

(c) If you have to take a telephone message, prepare yourself with a pen or pencil that works and plenty of paper. Be prepared to write in abbreviated note form – there is no need to write in sentences and you can re-write your notes after the call.

(d) When you take a call and the caller wants someone or something not at hand, don't leave them hanging on. Tell them you will ring them back.

(e) When you are taking a telephone message for someone else, make sure you note:

- the caller's name and phone number
- the message, time and date of the call

Exercise 1 (j)

E

Your school or college has decided to appoint a duty student to answer one of the main office phones every afternoon. Because the duty student will change each day, you have been asked to devise a set of instructions or guidelines for students on telephone technique. Devise the guidelines to fit on one side of A4 size paper.

E

Exercise 1 (k)

The manager of the advertising agency you work for has asked you to be on stand-by for an important call from America concerning a new marketing project for the company. By five o'clock that day, the call has not been received. The manager has gone and you are just leaving when the phone rings. It's the call from America about the new project. At first you can hear the call reasonably well and he asks you to take a message. Then the voice begins to fade under crackling and general interference. What do you do? What should you already have done?

Helping others to contribute

In a discussion, some people do not find it easy to talk. This problem increases when the two speakers or members of a group do not know one another. In these circumstances some people feel shy and uneasy. They feel everything they say will be judged critically. They lack confidence and feel what they have to say is of little value.

Helping others to contribute is a skill in its own right. Here are some methods:

(a) help each member of the discussion to express their feelings, views or ideas on the subject by inviting them to speak.

'John, how do you feel about this idea: would you like to say something at this stage?'

(b) make sure each member of the discussion feels they have a right to an equal say.

'Remember, everyone here has a right to an opinion on this subject. Just speak up when you want to speak.'

(c) show an awareness of gender roles and language in discussion and avoid sexist terms.

'Which would you prefer, chairman or chairperson?'

You must remember to:

- avoid trying to impress others or dominate the discussion
- listen with the same attention to each member of the discussion
- use body language such as nods and smiles to support others as they talk
- supply words and phrases to help someone make a point
- give others time to finish expressing themselves, even though they may hesitate and sometimes struggle for the right word
- avoid interrupting

Remember: in oral work, listening is just as important as speaking.

Checking for understanding

During a discussion it is important to check your understanding of the points that are made. This helps you to follow the line of argument and keep track of ideas that arise. There are a number of strategies for doing this:

- stopping the discussion in order to express your view of what has been said
- asking others to confirm your understanding
- asking others to repeat or re-phrase the points they have made
- reflecting back on the discussion with a partner to check your understanding of points made
- offering a summary of the discussion to a partner or group of your peers
- planning in advance for review during the discussion

Here are some sound-bites that you can associate with checking and confirming understanding in discussion.

'Are you saying ... '
'Am I right in thinking what's been said is ... '
'Would this be a fair summary of what's been said so far ... ?'
'It seems to me there are three main points being made here ... '
'It would be useful at this stage to reflect on what has been said ... '

How many more can you add to this list?

Making sure you get your point across

Sometimes the points made in a discussion are not understood. This may be because:

- points were poorly expressed
- there was too much detail for others to follow and understand
- the language was too complex
- for unknown reasons the listeners were unable to follow the discussion

Checking for understanding helps to identify the need to communicate the same information again.

What you need to do

When communication breaks down through lack of understanding, it is necessary to re-express the points made in a language and detail that will be more readily understood.

Exercise 1 (I)

E

How would you manage *either* of the following two situations and how would you re-express your instructions?

(a) As a team leader you have been given the task of deciding the layout of a promotional leaflet designed to promote a new health care product. Introducing the task to the team you said:

'Our task is to produce a health care leaflet.'

After an hour's discussion nothing has been decided and it is clear that more than half the team have misunderstood the brief and are discussing the strengths and weaknesses of the product itself.

(b) You are a member of a team assembled to decide on a customer service programme to support the launch of a new home computer. From the beginning it is obvious that half the team know little or nothing about computers and the problems sometimes associated with using them. The team members must complete the task. How would you address this problem?

E **Exercise 1 (m)**

Draft a written brief outlining how you would address the problems presented by either of the above situations.

Evaluating contributions

You can evaluate your own and others' contributions to a discussion by:

(a) Observation

- is the contribution expressed in appropriate terms?
- is the tone, pitch and pace correct?
- do listeners understand the contribution/do they appear interested?
- does the contribution make sense and is it relevant?

(b) Recording

- because of the fleeting quality of oral work, video or tape recordings or even written notes made during a discussion can be very useful sources of evidence.

(c) Discussion and thinking about your skills

Discussion with a partner or small group of friends is a useful way of testing your opinions and assessment of your own and others' contributions. You can also use the video or tape-recorded evidence to help analyse the discussion for skills that need to be developed by individual members.

Remember: when you are discussing others' contributions, it is important to avoid destructive comments. It is generally more helpful to highlight the strengths and to talk of skills for development, rather than pick up on faults and weaknesses.

There is a chance to try a real evaluation in the Skills in Practice exercise at the end of this chapter.

Using the kind of information collected from above, you now have the task of determining how you will use that information to improve your own and others' contributions in the future. The following table offers one way of approaching this.

Planning for development		
Areas	**Strategies for improvement**	**Opportunities for re-evaluation**
Talking over the top of others	See video for evidence Make a point of letting others finish their contribution	Discussion on Homelessness next Easter Term
Making points not relevant to the topic	Make more detailed notes on intended contribution	Next group discussion on study skills

How would you plan for other areas which needed development? Try to devise an example to fill the last row in the grid.

Agreement on outcomes

At the end of discussion it is necessary to agree and note the outcome. Sometimes this can be the chairperson's job. At other times the group appoints a secretary to list the main points as they arise and read them back for agreement at the end. This helps to:

- remind participants of key issues agreed
- indicate what was covered and what has still to be covered in discussion
- set future targets and agendas for further discussions

Exercise 1 (n)

E

Imagine you have attended a meeting of students and tutors on the subject of setting up a student council in your school or college. Present an oral summing up of:

- main points covered
- key issues agreed
- issues for future meetings

You could also present a written summary of the essential points made in the meeting.

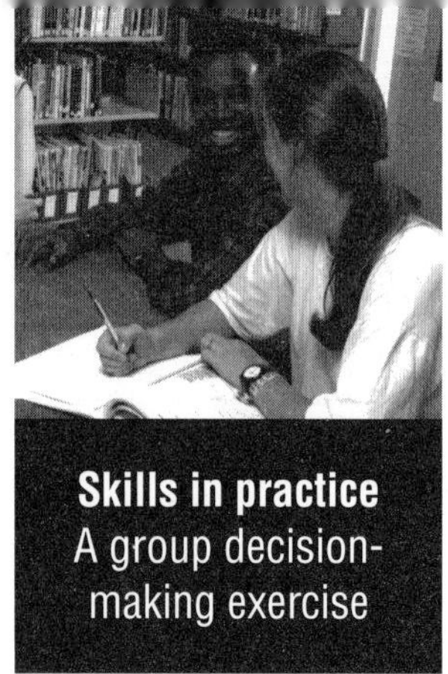

Skills in practice
A group decision-making exercise

The right person for the job

E

Exercise 1 (o)

Working in a group

Read right through the exercise instructions before beginning. Working in a group of four, the task is to decide which two of the four 'applicants' should be interviewed for the job of traffic warden. You have twenty minutes to make the decision.

Here are some tips:

- decide who is going to lead the group
- decide who is going to make notes
- each group member should make sure everyone takes part in speaking and listening
- express your own ideas, comments, examples, etc.
- allow others to have their say
- support or question the contributions of others
- discourage anyone who does not take it seriously

You can assume all applicants have received and read a full job description with information and guidance on how to apply for the post.

The following points may help you reach a decision:

(a) *Previous Work Experience*
A steady work record with good time-keeping and ability to deal with the public are important. All new recruits receive full training.

(b) *Qualifications*
A warden should have the ability to communicate effectively in speaking and reading and have some knowledge of mathematics or experience of working with figures.

(c) *Health*
Good physical health is important. All prospective wardens must pass a detailed medical examination.

(d) *Convictions and Motoring Offences*
A very serious view would be taken of any conviction relating to serious crime such as drink-driving, drugs, fraud, or violence.

(e) *Equal Opportunity*
Remember it is unfair and unlawful to discriminate against an applicant on the grounds of their gender, marital status, ethnic origin, race, colour, religion, nationality, or disability.

Exercise 1 (p)

E

Presenting your findings to an audience

One member of your group should present your choices. Your spokesperson will need to explain the reasons behind the group's selection. For this, he/she will need to use notes made during the decision-making and refer to the above headings as a guide. It will help to revise the skills section on the importance of tone and using speed and volume of voice correctly.

When presenting your findings, you should :

- plan your talk and give it an effective opening and ending
- use your voice and body effectively (see skills)
- be prepared to respond to comments and questions

If you are not presenting, write a commentary on each of the presenters. Comment on:

- body language
- how organised the talk was
- tone and manner of delivery
- how well they answered questions

Exercise 1 (q)

E

Answering questions – a role play exercise

Devise a role play in which the two successful applicants are interviewed for the post of warden. Two or more students can form the interview panel. It would be helpful if all students read each candidate's written details again before the actual interview.

The following points should help with the interview:

(a) Think carefully about the layout of the interview room/space.
Is each candidate going to face the interviewing panel across a table? Can the furniture be arranged differently? Does it matter?

(b) Decide on the questions before the interview. Will they be open questions, e.g., 'Tell us about your previous work experience?' or closed ' Did you enjoy your last job?'

(c) Think of ways of finding out how each candidate will react under pressure.

(d) Don't forget to give each candidate the opportunity to ask you questions.

Candidate 1

Name:	Paul Johnson
Age:	48
Ethnic Origin:	White European
Marital Status:	Married
Country of Birth:	England
Post Applied for:	Warden

Summary of application details:

Paul left school aged sixteen and worked for one year as a general hand in a local factory. At twenty Paul joined the Marines and spent tours of duty in Germany, Northern Ireland and Cyprus. After his apprenticeship in the Marines, Paul qualified as a skilled mechanic; a job he enjoyed for his twenty years' service.

Described by his Commanding Officer as a popular and likeable soldier with a great sense of humour, Paul has been unable to find a suitable job since retiring from the forces last Christmas.

Following an incident outside a public house on Christmas Eve two years ago, Paul was charged and fined for drunk and disorderly conduct.

Paul has a clean driving licence.

Candidate 2

Name: Jacky Taylor
Age: 38
Ethnic Origin: White European
Marital Status: Married
Country of Birth: England
Post Applied for: Warden

Summary of application details:

After leaving school, Jacky began a career as a clerical assistant in an insurance office where she learnt typing and secretarial skills. Jacky left to have her first of three children. Now that her children are all at secondary school, Jacky wishes to return to full-time employment and looks forward to the challenge of a new career.

Jacky really enjoys meeting people and says she is good at calming hot tempers. Jacky has one endorsement on her driving licence for speeding at 50 mph in a 30 mph zone which happened when she was rushing to collect her daughter from school on a wet afternoon. Jacky's father worked as a traffic warden for 15 years.

Candidate 3

Name: James Bradman
Age: 38
Ethnic Origin: Black Caribbean
Marital Status: Married
Country of Birth: England
Post Applied for: Warden

Summary of application details:

James began his career as a postman, but left after three years when he found the work unsuitable. James then worked for a private bus company at the weekends, taking single-decker coach tours to Bournemouth and Brighton.

Since his employers went bankrupt two years ago, James has been unable to find a suitable job and is keen to become a warden.

At the moment James works as a volunteer driver for Oxfam delivering bags of clothes to various shops around the country.

James has no convictions or fines. However, his former employers have remarked on his poor time-keeping and difficulty with figures.

Candidate 4

Name: Atikar Sharma
Age: 56
Ethnic Origin: Asian
Marital Status: Married
Country of Birth: Bangladesh
Post Applied for: Warden

Summary of application details:

Atikar has spent all of his working life as a school attendance officer and has just retired.

Although Atikar is enjoying his early retirement, he would like to be earning an income to support his two daughters at university. Atikar likes working with the public and has lots of experience dealing with difficult adults. He is good with figures.

In 1978 Atikar received a bravery award from the police for preventing a serious assault on a security guard during a robbery.

2

Getting it in writing

In this chapter you will:

- get to know about the purpose of your writing and those who read it
- revise the rules of correct spelling, punctuation and grammar
- get to know about the importance of presentation
- look at the range of writing forms you are expected to use

Your writing and your audience

In school the audience reading your work will mostly be teachers, fellow students or examiners. The same is true in college and higher education, although some of your college work may be read by people in the world of work beyond college.

When you leave school and college, written work you produce may be read by people who are unknown to you. For example:

- an application for a driving licence or passport
- the letters or reports you write on behalf of a company or organisation
- a research assignment for a company or university

You may also be asked to produce written work quickly and in ways you have not experienced much in school.

Getting to know these different forms of writing and when to use them are important communication skills your GNVQ will help you develop.

When we write it is usually for an *audience* and a *purpose*. This is true even if we are writing a diary for just ourselves to read. Read the following table in which the *audience* and *purpose* are linked to different forms of writing:

Form of writing	Audience	Purpose
An application letter for a job	Employer	To get a job
A short story	Readers	To amuse or give pleasure
A newspaper article	Readers	To inform, interest, or amuse
An exam paper	Students	To test ability
Instructions for using a video player	User	Instruct and inform
The Highway Code	Learner drivers	Instruct and inform
A holiday brochure	Holiday seekers	Give information and choice of holiday

Exercise 2 (a)

Can you tell the *purpose* and *audience* for these forms of writing?

Form of writing	Audience	Purpose
A school report		
Letter to an agony aunt		
A pamphlet on animal rights		
A train timetable		
A horoscope in a magazine		
A recipe for a sponge cake		
A CV for a job vacancy		
A record of achievement		

The range of formats

For all Levels – Foundation, Intermediate and Advanced – you are expected to be able to prepare written materials on given formats such as worksheets, forms, report forms, record cards and memoranda.

The following pages tell you about these formats and about the rules of writing that go with them.

A *format* is the way a page is set out for written material.

A *given format* means a number of headings and spaces are printed on the page ready to receive the written material. This makes it easy to fill in and easy to read. It helps the writer and the reader.

The language of formats

The language of formats often consists of broken sentences and words and phrases without formal punctuation. This is because headings are used in order to express information quickly and in the simplest form for everyone to read and follow easily. For example, an application form for a job with headings and spaces for personal information:

Name --

Address --

Date of birth --

Another example is a record card which looks like this:

Book title	Borrower	Department	Date out	Date returned

You may find a card like this in use in a college or school library. It is a quick and easy way of keeping track of books borrowed.

The quality of your writing (or what is called the *performance criteria*)

- For all Levels – Foundation, Intermediate and Advanced – the writing you produce needs to:
  - be clear, accurate and complete
  - have correct spelling, punctuation and grammar
- For Intermediate and Advanced Levels, the writing you produce **also** needs to be:
  - produced in a format which matches the material
  - organised in a way that makes it easy to follow and understand

Spelling, punctuation and grammar

Spelling

Clear and accurate writing needs correct spelling. If you are a weak speller, what can you do? Here is an interesting story.

A teacher, fed up correcting spelling mistakes, promised her class of twenty students she would give each one a five pound note if they handed in their next homework assignment without a single spelling mistake. She received twenty assignments free of errors. When asked how they came by this sudden ability to spell, most students admitted they'd checked every word with a dictionary. Some admitted they got someone else to check it for them. A few produced theirs on a computer, spell-checking their work before printing it.

'That proves one thing,' said the teacher, 'You may not be great spellers, but you can all produce good spelling when you really want to.'

The important thing to remember is that you can almost always get your spellings correct, provided you are prepared to put some effort into it.

Correct spelling depends upon:

- your natural ability to spell
- the methods you use to produce your writing and check your spelling
- how well you know the rules of spelling

- how adventurous you are with words
- the aids you use to remember spelling

Even if you are a strong speller, you will still have to check your work carefully for mistakes.

Spelling and the process of accurate writing

After brainstorming and planning your ideas, producing a rough draft is the next important step towards accurate writing. Even short pieces of writing may need to be drafted, especially when it has to be accurate. The rough draft allows you to:

- express your ideas freely without worrying too much about the spelling and punctuation
- be adventurous with words and meanings
- not worry about being criticised for making mistakes

Rough drafts are usually full of crossings out, false starts and changes. Most professional fiction writers produce at least one rough draft of a short story or novel. Some writers produce dozens.

When you are satisfied with your rough draft, you are ready to produce a good copy. The creative work is finished for the moment. This is when you become a checker. The next part is hard work and involves real effort. There is no short cut.

To check your spellings you should:

(a) Use a good dictionary – one or two you feel comfortable using which give you the kind of information you want. For example, some dictionaries not only list the spelling and meaning , but also the word family with *ed*, *ing* and *ly* endings.

(b) If you prefer, use an electronic spell checker which is quicker to use than a dictionary. They are more expensive and do not give you as much information as a dictionary, but are really fast at finding the correct spelling, even when the best you can do is make a rough guess at the word you want.

(c) Begin with the idea that you have probably made some spelling mistakes and then work towards finding them: don't give your writing the benefit of the doubt.

(d) Keep a list in a notebook of those spellings you get wrong. These will become your spelling targets and the notebook your spelling dictionary. Study your mistakes. Is there a pattern? Is there a way of remembering them in future?

(e) Try reading your sentences back to front as a way of making familiar words unfamiliar. This can help spot mistakes your mind skips through familiarity.

(f) Read your writing aloud. This often highlights mistakes the eye misses when sight reading.

What method do you use most to check your spelling and get your writing accurate and correct? How do you think you could improve your spelling?

Some useful spelling rules

You will understand the rules of spelling if you get to know these terms.

Vowels: The vowels are a, e, i, o, u.

Consonants: The consonants are all the other letters of the alphabet.

Prefix: A beginning added to a word to form a new word. For example:

dis + solve = dissolve
un + natural = unnatural
un + happy = unhappy

Suffix: An ending added to a word to form a new word. For example:

wonder + ful = wonderful
care + less = careless
use + less = useless

Syllable: A syllable is a single speech sound. For example:

One or single syllable words – run, sun, map.
Two-syllable words – believe, money, comfort.
Three-syllable words – assignment, remember, amusement.
Four-syllable words – television, necessary, replaceable.

The i before e rule

You may know about the *i before e except after c* rule. For example: believe, receive, deceive, relieve. There is another part to this rule which is less well known.

If you want to make an ee sound then it's i before e except after c.
For example:

field
shield
brief
belief
piece

If you want to make an a or i sound then it's e before i. For example:

eight
height
freight
neighbour

There are some exceptions. For example: weird, seize and some names like Keith and Sheila.

Exercise 2 (b) E

Write out the following putting 'ei' or 'ie' in the the blank spaces.

(a) I find that very hard to bel _ _ ve.
(b) There was a fly on the c _ _ ling.
(c) The student said it was a rel _ _ f to finish the assignment.
(d) The lady in the library said we had to be qu _ _ t.
(e) Passing my driving test was a great ach _ _ vement.
(f) Where we live, there is a N _ _ ghbourhood Watch scheme.
(g) They decided to measure the h _ _ ght of the fence.
(h) After Christmas he went on a d _ _ t to try and loose w _ _ ght.
(i) We went to the l _ _ sure centre for a swim.
(j) The aud _ _ nce left the theatre quickly after the show.

When to change y to i

Rule: If you add a suffix to a word which ends in a consonant followed by y, the y must change to i. For example:

happy + ness = happiness
empty + ness = emptiness
apply + ed = applied

Try adding your own suffixes to the following words:

necessary, qualify, ugly, beauty, occupy

Plurals

(a) If a single noun ends in y, look at the letter before the y; if it's a consonant, change the y to *ies* to form the plural. For example:

lady = ladies family = families fairy = fairies

Exercise 2 (c) E

Try changing these to their plural form:

- penny
- battery
- journey
- spy
- salary
- jelly
- holiday
- monkey
- worry
- baby

(b) Plural of nouns ending in o

If a single noun ends in the letter o, look at the letter before the o. If it is a consonant, add *es*. For example:

potato = potatoes echo = echoes domino = dominoes

Some exceptions are: photos, dynamos, kilos

If the letter before the o is a vowel, just add s. For example:

studio = studios stereo = stereos cargo = cargoes

E

Exercise 2 (d)

Try changing these to their plural form:

◆ buffalo ◆ torpedo ◆ tomato ◆ video ◆ hero ◆ kangaroo ◆ volcano ◆ radio

Prefixes

A prefix is added to the beginning of a word to change or extend its meaning. Here are some of the most common.

auto (meaning self) e.g. autobiography, automatic, autograph.

dis (meaning not or without) e.g. disappear, dissolve, dissatisfied.

inter (meaning between or among) e.g. interchange, international, intercom.

mis (meaning mistaken or wrong) e.g. misbehave, misfire, misfortune, mishap.

pre (meaning before) e.g. precede, present, prefer, predict.

super (meaning above or outside) e.g. superior, supermarket, supernatural.

sub (meaning under or further) e.g. submarine, subconscious, subdivide.

trans (meaning across or beyond) e.g. transfer, transport, transform, translate.

un (meaning not or the reverse) e.g. unhappy, unlikely, uncover, unusual, undo.

These prefixes are sometimes spelled incorrectly:

anti (meaning against) e.g. antiseptic, antifreeze.

ante (meaning before) e.g. antechamber, antenatal.

bi (meaning two or twice) e.g. bicycle, bifocals, bikini.

co (meaning together or associated) e.g. cooperative, cooperate.

When you want to create the opposite meaning to a word, you have a choice of several different prefixes. For example:

un + necessary = unnecessary	il + legal = illegal
im + possible = impossible	ir + rational = irrational

When you use the prefix *dis* (meaning not or without) with a word which begins with s, remember to kept the letter s in dis. For example:

satisfied + dis = dissatisfied	solve + dis = dissolve

When you add 'all' to the beginning of a word, use one l. For example:

all + was = always	all + together = altogether
all + ready = already	all + most = almost

Exercise 2 (e)

E

Add prefixes to these words to create new words or words of opposite meaning:

◆ play ◆ embark ◆ usual ◆ easy ◆ appear ◆ regular ◆ natural ◆ agree
◆ pleasure ◆ service ◆ similar ◆ appoint ◆ climax ◆ monthly ◆ clockwise

Suffixes

A suffix is added to the end of a word to change or extend its meaning. Here are some of the most common and the spelling rules that go with them:

(a) If you add a suffix beginning with a vowel to a word ending in e, you drop the e. For example:

ed – hope + ed = hoped
move + ed = moved
picture + ed = pictured

ing – smoke + ing = smoking
care + ing = caring
amuse + ing = amusing

ion – educate + ion = education
relate + ion = relation

ous – nerve + ous = nervous

But note these exceptions:

courageous sizeable

(b) The suffixes *ise* and *ize*

With most words you have a choice of using either *ise* or *ize*. For example:

organise or organize, criticise or criticize, realise or realize. Some people prefer *ize* because it is closer to the original Greek *izo* from which this ending is derived. But some words have to be spelled with *ise* because the origin is not Greek. For example, 'supervise' comes from super + the Latin *visus* meaning seen (to oversee or manage). Which is why if you use *ise* you will always be right.

Other words which must use *ise* include:

advertise compromise revise expertise
advise enterprise precise disguise

(c) The suffixes *ery*, *ary* and *ory*

The suffix *ery* is usually added to a root word which can stand on its own without the suffix. For example:

slip + ery = slippery snob + ery = snobbery
nurse + ery = nursery

But note these exceptions: mystery, stationery, surgery, cemetery.

The suffixes *ary* and *ory* are usually part of the root word which cannot stand alone without the suffix. For example:

library February laboratory ordinary

(d) The suffixes *able* and *ible*

The suffix *able* is used after root words that stand on its own. For example:

love + able = lovable (the *e* is dropped as above)
remove + able = removable
value + able = valuable

The suffix *ible* is used after a part of a word which cannot stand alone. For example:

possible visible legible sensible

When you use 'full' as a suffix, it loses an 'l' and becomes 'ful'. For example:

beauty + full = beautiful
shame + full = shameful
faith + full = faithful
pain + full = painful

Some helpful suffix rules

(a) When you add a suffix beginning with a vowel to a one-syllable word ending with a vowel and a consonant, you double the last letter. For example:

slip + ing = slipping
plan + ing = planning
beg + ar = beggar
fit + ing = fitting

(b) When you add a suffix beginning with a consonant to a one-syllable word ending with a vowel and a consonant, you do not change the word. For example:

sad + ly = sadly
wit + ness = witness
skin + less = skinless

E ***Exercise 2 (f)***

Add suffixes to these words to create new words or extend the meaning:

- forget
- limit
- require
- allot
- target
- travel
- gallop
- marvel
- small
- equal
- civil
- appear
- permit
- present
- friend
- discover
- final
- skill
- extract
- repeat
- sorrow
- transfer
- access

Some verb and noun endings

Some words sound the same but have entirely different meanings and end with a c or s depending on whether they are nouns or verbs. For example:

Verbs	**Nouns**
practise	practice
devise	device
advise	advice
license	licence

'The team have a practice every Saturday morning. They practise their passing skills.'

'The tutor gave the student some good advice. She was advised to stop smoking.'

'She passed her test and got a licence. Unfortunately she was not licensed to drive a heavy goods vehicle.'

Some tips for remembering spellings

What about words you always seem to get wrong? One way of remembering the correct spelling is to invent a *mnemonic* or memory aid. Mnemonic is a Greek word and is pronounced nemonics without the m. Follow these steps:

- look closely at the word you got wrong and compare it to the correct spelling
- what exactly was wrong with your spelling?
- what do you need to remember about that word?
- write the correct word and highlight the letters you need to remember
- invent a memory aid or mnemonic

For example: suppose you misspell separate as seperate. You could remember the correct word with :

There's *a rat* in sep*arat*e.

or

You misspell sincerely as sincerly. Try –

You need *two e*ars to be sincere.

Sometimes finding another word within a word is useful. For example:

A *secret*ary can keep a *secret*.
Bu*sin*ess can be a *sin*.

Inventing a rhyme or funny sentence is another way of remembering the correct order of letters in a word:

weird **e**lephants **i**n **r**ed **d**resses

Try inventing your own mnemonics for the words you always seem to get wrong.

E

Exercise 2 (g)

During his apprenticeship as a boat builder, John had an accident which left him unfit for heavy work. John decided to retrain for clerical work and went to college to gain some further qualifications. At school John's spelling was always his greatest weakness. Now at college his lack of confidence in his spelling made him feel inferior and ashamed. John tried to keep it a secret and used simple words which did not show his true ability to think and understand.

What advice would you give to John or any student in his position? Make a list of your suggestions.

Punctuation

The apostrophe

The apostrophe is a mark like a comma that sits just above the letters of a word.

e.g. woman's

The main purpose of the apostrophe is to show that a letter or letters have been left out. For example:

It's a bright day = It is a bright day
We'll see you later = We will see you later
I don't know where she's gone = I do not know where she has gone

The second use is to show that something belongs to someone. For example:

My mother's coat is on the chair = the coat belonging to the mother
Peter's assignment is on the table = the assignment belonging to Peter
The driver's foot was on the brake = the foot belonging to the driver

E

Exercise 2 (h)

Fill in the apostrophe in these examples:

(a) My sisters friend is having a party.
(b) Paulines piano lesson lasted an hour.
(c) The mechanic said the cars engine needed new plugs.
(d) The childrens laughter could be heard at the bottom of the stairs.
(e) The tutors files were on the desks at the front of the room.
(f) The doctors number was in Joans notebook.

When *not* is shortened with another word, the apostrophe always replaces the o. For example:

did not = didn't   were not = weren't   should not = shouldn't
have not = haven't   will not = won't   can not = can't
had not = hadn't

Exercise 2 (i)

Write the short form for each of these:

(a) I did not know his name.
(b) The cat is sitting on the table.
(c) They will have no idea where to look.
(d) The time is not right.
(e) We were not in the room at the time.

When you want to show possession and the possessor does not end in s then add apostrophe s. For example:

men – the men's room
car – the car's wheels
girl – the girl's bicycle

When the possessor ends in s then just add an apostrophe. For example:

students – the students' accommodation (belonging to more than one student)
ladies – the ladies' toilet

If a person's name ends in 's', e.g. James, then just add an apostrophe or an apostrophe + s. For example:

King James' Castle
Tess's dress
Archimedes' principle

The apostrophe is also used for words which do not normally have a plural form. For example:

How many c's in necessary?
Remember to dot your i's and cross your t's.

The colon : and semicolon ;

The colon is used to introduce a number of items. For example:

The table was set with: fresh fruit, cheese, wine, cake, fresh strawberries, cold meats.

The semicolon is used to join two statements that are connected. It is not as strong as a full stop, but stronger than a comma. For example:

The table was set for tea; fresh bread and salad formed the main course.

The comma

The comma is used to show a short pause in a sentence. For example:

When John entered the room, he was really surprised at the new furniture.

The comma is also used to separate items on a list. For example:

The shopping list consisted of: eggs, bacon, soft drink and coffee.

The hyphen

The hyphen is used to join two words together in order when:

(a) There may be misunderstanding with some words, e.g. re-sign

'The manager decided to re-sign the player'
but
'The player decided to resign.'

(b) Compound words are formed, e.g. ice-cold, left-handed, full-bodied, good-sized, man-eating

(c) A prefix is added to a noun or adjective which begins with a capital letter, e.g. anti-Christian, pro-Russian

Grammar

Grammar is a set of rules to help us understand how we may use language. Grammar does not describe everything about the English language, which has many exceptions to its own rules and is always changing and evolving. This section explains what grammar is and how it will help your writing.

The first thing to know about grammar is that you are always using it. For example, take a simple sentence like:

'I went to the cinema yesterday.'

This makes sense. But did you know it contains a personal pronoun, preposition, definite article, past tense of a verb and two nouns ? These are called *parts of speech* and there are rules on how they relate to one another and where they should come in a sentence. Getting to know the parts of speech is one part of understanding how the language works. It is helpful to know because:

- it can help us name and identify our mistakes
- it keeps us on the right lines when we are writing for others to read
- it can help us to understand what we may need to do to improve how we use language for different tasks

The parts of speech

There are several parts of speech. Here are some of the more important ones:

(a) Nouns

Nouns are the words we use to name things. There are basically four different types of nouns:

- common nouns: which are the names of common things like road, bicycle, table, chair, machine
- abstract nouns: the names we give to ideas such as beauty, joy, hate, fear, knowledge
- proper nouns: names of places and people, e.g. France, London, Karen, Bill
- collective nouns: words we use to describe groups of things or people, e.g. flock (of sheep), swarm (of bees), team (of footballers)

(b) Pronouns

These words take the place of nouns. (I, you, he, she, him, them, their, it, his, her). Generally they make speaking and writing much quicker and stop you having to repeat the same words. For example:

'Mrs Makepiece turned the handle, stepped forward and entered the room' could be – 'She opened the door and went in.'

'Mary plays the piano twice a day' could be – 'She plays it twice a day.'

Exercise 2 (j) E

Try changing the nouns to pronouns in these sentences:

(a) Carol decided it was a good idea to leave the puppies alone.
(b) London is always crowded at this time of the day.
(c) The principal spoke to the students in private.
(d) Mr Johnson asked if he could travel to France by rail.

(c) Adjectives

Adjectives are words used to describe or tell you more information about nouns or pronouns. There are four types of adjective:

(a) Asking or interrogative adjectives.

Which assignment will you finish first?
What kind of coffee do you drink?

(b) Possessive adjectives. These show ownership.

He went to his locker and got *his* lunch.
Joan never liked *my* cooking.

(c) Adjectives which describe numbers or quantity.

Over *two hundred* sheep in one truck.
There wasn't *enough* food in the cupboard.

(d) Adjectives which point something or someone out.

Those people are in a hurry.
That mirror belongs to this car.

Exercise 2 (k) E

Underline the adjectives in these sentences:

(a) A yellow building with square windows.
(b) The small tree in a large garden.
(c) He was frightened of the dark.
(d) There are five ships in the harbour.
(e) She is the tallest girl in the college.
(f) That painting is the most beautiful of all her works.

(d) Verbs

A verb is the word used to describe an action or state of being:

John *drank* his coffee.
The tutor *signed* the project folder.
She *swam* over three hundred metres.
He *worked* all night to mend the nets.
Peter *wished* for a long holiday.

Tense

Verbs change according to the tense they express. The tense tells you when the action takes place.

Consider these examples:

Subject	Present	Past	Future
I	wait	waited	shall wait
you (singular)	wait	waited	will wait
he/she/it	waits	waited	will wait
we	wait	waited	shall wait
you (plural)	wait	waited	will wait
they	wait	waited	will wait

E **Exercise 2 (I)**

List the tenses of the following verbs:

◆ believe ◆ eat ◆ swim ◆ study

(e) Adverbs

Adverbs usually tell you more about the verb and there are several kinds:

- manner: happily, quickly, well
  He ran quickly to attend the accident.
- place: down, here, there, up
  She walked near the river.
- time: now, soon, then today
  It will happen today before noon.
- frequency: never, always, often, occasionally
  Tom never opened his mouth.
- sentence: definitely, surely, certainly
  I certainly hope she finishes her assignment.

- degree: rather, too, very, hardly
  The officer hardly looked at the bag.
- interrogative: when, where, why
  Where is the map?
- relative: when, where, why
  This is the year when he was born

(f) Prepositions

Prepositions are words which show how a person or thing relates to another person or thing. For example: to, for, at, on, by, before, in, during, beside, since, for, off, out, above.

The child is *with* his mother.
The file is *under* the desk.
Jennie sits *beside* Mary *at* the front of the room.

Although prepositions are always attached to a noun or pronoun, they are sometimes used with verbs to give them a special or new meaning:

'The crowd suddenly charged into the stadium' but
'The driver was ***charged with*** *careless driving.'*

'He hopes to pass his exam this year' but
'They decided to ***pass over*** *the forest before coming in to land.'*

Prepositions are also used as adverbs:

'The fireman climbed ***up*** *the ladder.'*

Here the preposition 'up' tells you about the relationship between the fireman and the ladder, but
'The fireman climbed ***up****.'*

Here 'up' is an adverb which tells you where the fireman climbed.

Exercise 2 (m)

Underline the prepositions in these sentences:

(a) Joan got up late because she was on holiday.
(b) He said he believed in ghosts.
(c) Paul could not decide whether to stay or to go.
(d) She lived on fruit and water for a week.

(g) Conjunctions

Conjunctions are connecting words used to join other words and parts of a sentence together. For example: and, but, both, either, however, nevertheless, otherwise, still, yet, unless, although.

She is a good sleeper *but* a poor riser.
There is good *and* bad in us all.
This is what happens *when* you run out of petrol.

Conjunctions also appear in pairs joining parts of a sentence:

He smokes *and* drinks *but* never during the week.
Ron plays *not only* football, *but also* tennis and cricket.
Paul was *neither* at college *nor* at home.

E

Exercise 2 (n)

Fill in the missing conjunctions in these sentences:

(a) He set the table ______________ plates, cups ______________ saucers, bread rolls ______________ a pot of coffee.

(b) She could not decide ______________ to wear her black dress ______________ her leggings ______________ shirt.

(c) Paul waited for the bus ______________ it was well past the arrival time.

(d) You can swim ______________ only after the children have left the pool.

Fill in the missing pairs of conjunctions in these sentences:

(e) You can ______________ walk to the top ______________ catch the train.

(f) Peter broke ______________ the handbrake ______________ the light switch.

(g) The group had to make a decision ______________ to stay on the mountain ______________ return to base.

(h) The police could not decide ______________ it was true ______________ false.

The importance of presentation

Printed and handwritten

Using a word processor, typewriter or personal computer is one way of producing writing that is neat and legible. If your handwriting style is difficult to read, producing written work in this way becomes even more important. Word processing also makes drafting, redrafting and editing the work easier as well. Yet some work, like personal letters and some assignments, are still best handwritten.

Why do you think certain forms of writing are best printed?

Is it because:

- it is neater and more pleasing to the eye?
- it can be read more easily?
- there will be fewer mistakes?
- most people have difficulty reading handwriting?
- you can get more words on the page?

Exercise 2 (o)

E

Which of these forms of writing would you expect to be handwritten and which would you expect to be in print? Can you explain why?

(a) A personal letter to a close relative
(b) A statement from a witness taken at the scene of an accident
(c) A police notice warning about leaving valuables in your car
(d) A GNVQ main subject assignment
(e) A Curriculum Vitae
(f) A surveyor's report on a house for sale
(g) The rough draft of a speech

Deciding when to use handwriting and when to print or word process your work depends on a number of factors:

- **what is expected or required by the reader**

  for example: a tutor who wants an assignment produced using IT equipment, **or** an intimate friend who expects a handwritten letter.

- **the demands of the situation or context**

  for example: a police officer writing down a witness statement at the scene of a road accident, **or** a quickly typed memo sent to all building society branches giving accurate information on stolen cash books.

- **the needs of the reader or audience**

  for example: a typed or word processed story sent to a magazine where the editor reads many hundreds of stories a week, **or** a handwritten comment on a get well card sent to friend in hospital.

Filling in forms

Many pre-set or given formats are expected to be filled in using handwriting. For example:

Passport application
Job application
Social Security documents
Mortgage and bank account application
Travel warrant application
Student loan or grant forms
Telephone message notes

are all examples of forms which require handwriting.

The important thing is to be clear and correct.

Some tips for filling in forms:

- Read the instructions on the form carefully.
- Does the instruction ask for CAPITAL or BLOCK LETTERS?

- Read the entire form carefully before you begin to write.
- Photocopy the form and use the copy as a first draft.
- If you make a mistake, cross it out neatly and add correction.
- Avoid using correcting fluid, it can be messy.
- Delete means put a neat line through (a word or phrase alternative).
- If you are asked to tick a box, there is only one form of tick and it looks like this ✔. A box which has been ticked looks like this – ☑.

Work on formats

E Exercise 2 (p)

The following examples are in given formats. Study these formats and try to answer these questions:

(a) Why do the headings cover a range of situations or possibilities?
(b) Why are the headings short and to the point?
(c) What do you think are the strengths and weaknesses of these formats?
(d) How do you see these type of formats developing and changing in the future?

Example A

MESSAGE

To: ______________________

Date: ____________ Time ____________

WHILE YOU WERE OUT

M ______________________

of ______________________

Phone No. ______________________

☐ TELEPHONED ☐ PLEASE CALL

☐ WAS IN TO SEE YOU ☐ WILL CALL BACK

☐ WANTS TO SEE YOU

☐ RETURNED YOUR CALL ☐ *URGENT*

____
____
____
____
____
____
____
____
____
____

Message taken by ______________________

Example B

Requisition for rail ticket/warrant

Name ______________________

Department ______________________

Location ______________________

Company ______________________

Departure from ______________________

Destination ______________________

____

Date of journey out ______________________

Date of journey in ______________________

Single/return ______________________

First/second class ______________________

Standard/Cheap Day/network/ saver/weekly season

Authorised by

____

Memoranda

The purpose of a memorandum, or memo as it is often called, is to send a quick message of information within an organisation or business. Memos are intended to be informal notes between colleagues, which is why the greetings which you find in a normal letter are not necessary. The memo outline is simple and contains an outline space for:

- the name of the sender (which is at the beginning)
- the name of the receiver
- the date sent
- a brief message

The format looks like this:

MEMORANDUM

To: From:

Date:

____

Completed it may look like this:

MEMORANDUM

To: *Sonia Herson* From: *Hugh Johnson*

Date: *12th Dec*

I need to examine the stock cupboards before next Friday.

Please suggest a date and time for examination.

Since the introduction of computer networks, electronic messages or EMs, have increasingly replaced the internal memo as a short and quick means of communication. For this form of message the computer creates its own pre-set format and, like the traditional paper memo, it's simply a task of filling in the spaces.

E **Exercise 2 (q)**

Pre-set or given formats

(a) How many examples of pre-set formats can you find in use in your college, school or work environment?

(b) How often do you use pre-set formats?

(c) What do you consider to be the qualities of a good pre-set format?

(d) What do you think are the advantages and disadvantages of electronic memos?

E **Exercise 2 (r)**

You have been asked to design a pre-set format for use in your college, school or work place. The purpose of the format is to report on accidents that occur on the premises. In the event of an accident, reports will be sent to the head or principal, but copies may be read by insurance companies, the police or courts at a later date. You are asked to include these sections:

(a) time and date of accident

(b) name of person injured

(c) nature of injury and cause

(d) place of accident

(e) how the accident happened and who or what was responsible

(f) name and address of witness(es)

(g) name of medic attending or name of hospital where injured was sent

(h) time and date of report.

Points to remember:

- You will find it helpful to obtain a few examples of actual accident report forms and study their layouts before you begin this exercise.
- Your report format may be used by anyone who enters the premises, (accidents can happen to anyone and anyone can witness one) including young children, senior citizens, foreign visitors, students.
- Presentation – a format of this kind is best produced on a word processor, where it is possible to combine headings with lines and boxes to produce a professional final copy.
- Although your report is for the head or principal, a great many other people may read it or use it as evidence. How should this influence the language you use and the way you design and present your format?
- Should your format include any special instructions other than those listed above?

Exercise 2 (s)

E

Using IT equipment, design and create a memorandum. Send a copy to your main subject tutor(s) with the message that you are actively engaged in learning about memoranda and pre-set formats as part of your Core Skills Communications.

Before you send your memo test your format for quality. Remember the performance criteria at the beginning of this section. You could ask a friend or colleague to judge your work as well.

(a) Is your document clear, accurate and complete – have you included all the right information (see above)?

(b) Is your document legible? Can it be read by any of those mentioned above? If you have used a typewriter or word processor, you should have produced a format which is easily read by everyone.

(c) Have you used correct spelling, punctuation and grammar? Again, get someone else to proof read it for you. An unfamiliar eye often sees mistakes missed by the writer.

Further writing requirements

Above Foundation Level there are some extra requirements for writing:

For Intermediate and Advanced Levels you are **also** expected to prepare written material with *outline formats* such as letters, reports, entries in log books and your own material in which you decide on the outline.

Outline formats means page layouts where information is expected to appear in set places. For example, letters which have rules where the address, date, names etc. should be placed.

Letters, reports and log books

Outline formats refer to layouts such as letters, reports and log books on which information is placed in set places. In the following pages we will look at each of these in turn and get to know the skills used in producing them.

Letters

Letter writing is an everyday activity in business, industry and the professions. Many companies and organisations have special letter headings designed on which to send out their letters. A typical heading will consist of a firm's name, address, telephone and fax number and sometimes a logo which identifies the firm and helps advertise their name.

STONE MARK
Monumental Masons
The Old Forge, Countryside
Somewhere TS3 4RN
Telephone: 01435 678489
Fax: 01435 678423
CERAMIC TILES LTD
136 Commercial Road
Somechester
East Sussex
BN20 4SB
Tel: (01493) 657892
Fax: (01493) 657687

Apart from these special letter headings, letters have straightforward rules on outline format. Many people are anxious about getting the layout of a letter correct. Yet there is no one correct format, but a number of possible layouts.

Here are the four most common:

(a) This is called the *indented/punctuated*, because the address is written or printed in even steps (indents). Note how each line of the address except the postcode has commas at the end.

24 Fisherman's Row,
Fleets Bridge,
Bath,
Avon
BH16 6FB
15th Jan 1995

The Service Manager,
Customer Service Dept,
Table Lamps Ltd.,
Norwich,
Norfolk
NR5 5NL

Dear Sir,

I am writing to enquire about a new part for my table lamp which fell off the coffee table last week. Unfortunately the switch next to the stem broke in two pieces in the fall and I was wondering if it would be possible to replace it with the same type.
I realise this...

Yours faithfully,

John Scott

(b) This is called the *fully blocked/unpunctuated,* because all the lines are blocked to the left-hand margin. This is a format used frequently in business and it is quick and easy to produce. You do not have to worry about indenting or commas at the end of lines.

24 Fisherman's Road
Fleets Bridge
Bath
Avon
BH16 6FB

15th Jan 1995

The Service Manager
Customer Service Dept
Table Lamps Ltd.
Norwich
Norfolk
NR5 5NL

Dear Sir

I am writing to enquire about a new part for my table lamp which fell off the coffee table last week. Unfortunately the switch next to the stem broke in two pieces in the fall and I was wondering if it would be possible to replace it with the same type.
I realise this...

Yours faithfully

John Scott

(c) This is called *semi-blocked/punctuated*, because the address in the top right-hand corner is blocked. In all other respects it follows the same layout as **(a)**.

24 Fisherman's Row,
Fleets Bridge,
Bath,
Avon
BH16 6FB

15th Jan 1995

The Service Manager,
Customer Service Dept,
Table Lamps Ltd.,
Norwich,
Norfolk
NR5 5NL

Dear Sir,

I am writing to enquire about a new part for my table lamp which fell off the coffee table last week. Unfortunately the switch next to the stem broke in two pieces in the fall and I was wondering if it would be possible to replace it with the same type.
I realise this...

Yours faithfully,

John Scott

(d) This is called *semi-blocked/unpunctuated* and is the same as **(c)** except that there are no commas at the end of the address, after the opening salutation, or after the ending.

24 Fisherman's Row
Fleets Bridge
Bath
Avon
BH16 6FB

15th Jan 1995

The Service Manager
Customer Service Dept
Table Lamps Ltd.
Norwich
Norfolk
NR5 5NL

Dear Sir

I am writing to enquire about a new part for my table lamp which fell off the coffee table last week. Unfortunately the switch next to the stem broke in two pieces in the fall and I was wondering if it would be possible to replace it with the same type.
I realise this..

Yours faithfully

John Scott

<u>Remember: The only rule about using any of these formats is to be consistent. Decide on one and use it.</u>

A few other rules of letter writing

(a) Informal letters to friends, family and acquaintances *usually* follow outlines (a) or (c) but without the receiver's address by the left-hand margin. Informal letters are also often handwritten, although if your handwriting is difficult to read, a printed letter is better.

(b) When the letter begins with a name – e.g. Dear Mr. Jones – then you should end with *Yours sincerely*. For *Dear Madam* or *Dear Sir* you end with *Yours faithfully*.

(c) If you finish the main content of your letter on a page and need to use another page for *Yours sincerely* and the name, always carry the last paragraph onto the next page as well. This avoids awkward presentation.

(d) *Yours faithfully* and *Yours sincerely* always use a capital Y and a small f and s.

(e) Print your name under your signature and also follow this with your correct title in brackets, e.g. Mr., Miss, Dr., Ms.

(f) Like other prose material, each new subject within the body of the letter requires a new paragraph.

Exercise 2 (t) E

An exercise in letter writing – answer *(a)* or *(b)*

(a) As a student you are asked to conduct a survey on the travel arrangements of students coming to college. Write a letter to the principal of your college asking permission to conduct a three day survey for this. The aim of the survey is to discover the most common means of transport and the average distance travelled by students. The information will be used by you for further work in core skill Application of Numeracy and the *Working with images* section of your GNVQ Communications Studies. You will need to explain that the information will be kept strictly confidential and not used for any other purpose but your GNVQ assignment.

(b) As a student you are asked to conduct a survey on the travel arrangements of hospital day patients. Write a letter to the manager of your local hospital asking for permission to conduct a two day survey on day patients. The aim of the survey is to discover the average distance travelled by patients and the most common means of transport. You will need to explain that the information will be kept strictly confidential and not used for any other purpose but your GNVQ assignment.

Set out your letter carefully, using any one of the suitable outlines. You may find this paragraph plan helpful:

(a) Introduce yourself and explain briefly and in general terms why you are writing.
(b) Explain the aim of your project and why you need the information.
(c) Say what you hope to achieve from the survey.
(d) Reassure the reader that the information will be kept confidential.

(e) Express your thanks for their time and cooperation.

You could also include a sample format of how you intend to organise the recording of the survey information.

Remember: for business and formal communications, it is always better to type or word process your material.

Now test your letter for quality. Remember, you could ask a friend or colleague to judge your work instead.

- Is your letter complete and accurate – have you included all the right information?
- Is your letter legible? Remember, you could use a typewriter or word processor, especially if your handwriting is difficult to read.
- Does the language you have used follow the rules of correct spelling, punctuation and grammar? Again, get someone else to proof read it for you. An unfamiliar eye often sees mistakes missed by the writer.
- Is the outline used appropriate to the nature of the material and is the information organised so that it is easy to follow and understand?

Reports

Like other forms of writing, reports are written for different purposes and different audiences. A school report is intended to give student and parents information about progress and achievement. An AA report on a second-hand car is intended to give a customer a professional opinion and information about the mechanical condition of a car.

Remember: reports lead to action and help people make decisions.

E

Exercise 2 (u)

Define the *audience*, the *purpose* and the likely *action* following the reports below.

(a) An employer's report on a student's work experience placement in his/her company.
(b) A surveyor's report on a house for sale.
(c) An accountant's report on the financial state of a company.
(d) A safety officer's report on fire precautions in a theatre.
(e) An education inspector's report on a school.
(f) A *Which?* consumer magazine report on washing machines.
(g) A public health officer's report on a restaurant.

Routine and non-routine reports

There are two basic types of report – routine and non-routine. A *routine report* is a report that is produced regularly. For example:

- an auditor's report on a company's financial management
- a teacher's report on his student
- a road surveyor's annual report on a motorway

A *non-routine* report is one which is not expected regularly. For example:

- a police report on a road traffic accident
- a medical report on the outbreak of illness in a rest home
- an engineer's report on the collapse of a bridge

The main features of reports

The nature of reports will vary, from routine financial reports on companies, to complex non-routine reports by government officers on safety in a nuclear power station. The layout will vary too, yet all reports should have these common features: terms of reference, title, introduction, limitations, method, conclusions and recommendations. These are dealt with in detail in the following pages.

(a) Terms of Reference. This refers to:

- the main subject of the report
- the scope and purpose of the report
- the audience who will read it

The terms of reference should therefore tell you – *what* the report is going to discuss, *why* it is being produced and *who* will read it. You need to know this information before you begin the process of producing the report.

For a report the What + Why + Who = Terms of Reference

Exercise 2 (v)

E

Try to determine the *Terms of Reference* of these two examples:

(a) Following the failure of more than one hundred of their new model 300 series lawn mowers, Wessex Mowers employed an independent engineer to conduct a full investigation and present a report within a month.

(b) The principal of a large college wants a new computer system for the main administration block. She gives one of the IT tutors three days paid leave to research and investigate the best value for money on a system that will suit the college needs. The principal would like a report within two weeks.

(b) Title

Only when you have established the terms of reference are you in a position to think about a title. Take the example of the Wessex Mower report above. You will already have decided on the terms of reference. Which of these do you think is a suitable title for the report? Explain why.

(a) Failure of Wessex Mowers
(b) Failure of new model mower
(c) Failure in the new 300 series model mower
(d) The New 300 series mower – a report

As you can see, (c) is the most suitable title because it is the one which is true to the terms of reference. The other titles are too general and not direct enough. For a title to be of any value it must:

- be true to the terms of reference
- be precise and refer directly to the subject

(c) Introduction

Now that you have the title, you can write the introduction. An introduction has a number of different elements. For example:

- background to the report
- the purpose of the report
- how the report is generally structured
- who the report is for

For the report on *Failure in the new 300 series model mower*, the Introduction might be as follows:

> The purpose of this report is to advise the Wessex Mower company on the reason for failure in a large number of their new 300 series lawn mowers. The report was commissioned after the return to service centres and retailers of over one hundred of the 300 series models from dissatisfied customers.
>
> The first section of the report will deal with my research and findings. The second part will deal with my conclusions and recommendations.
>
> I examined over sixty returned models of this series and discovered two manufacturing faults which had caused failure.
>
> The first of these............etc

Note how the title is accurate and the introduction states the purpose, background, structure and who the report is for.

E **Exercise 2 (w)**

Try writing a *Title* and *Introduction* for the following report:

> Following a fire on the forecourt of one of their biggest motorway service stations, Pestco Oil have employed an independent fire inspector to investigate the cause and present a report. They want the report within two weeks.

Remember:

- first determine the *terms of reference* (what,why and who?)
- check that your *title* is precise and refers directly to the subject
- make sure your *introduction* includes the background, the purpose, who the report is for and the report's general structure

(d) Limitations

Reports are always written within a certain period of time and with a set amount of resources.

Remember: Reports lead to action and help people make decisions.

Often reports are needed urgently to correct the cause of a serious problem or to prevent future loss or injury. The Wessex Mower report is urgent because the information it contains could prevent accident or injury for which the company could be held liable in law.

The Pestco Oil Service Station report is also urgent because the information it contains could prevent a fire at another station.

A comment about the limitations on time and resources needs to be mentioned in the report. For example:

> I would have preferred to have examined all of the returned mowers and spoken to several retailers on the difficulties their customers experienced starting the machines. Unfortunately not all the mowers were available and time did not allow for visits to retailers.

Exercise 2 (x) E

Write a comment on limitations for the Pestco Oil Service Station report.

(e) Method

Looking back to the Wessex Mower report, you can see that the writer has started to explain his method:

> I examined over sixty returned models of this series and discovered two manufacturing faults which had caused failure.

The method is the way in which the person writing the report has chosen to research and investigate the subject. It is important to state the method because it lets the readers know exactly how the report has been conducted and how it meets the terms of reference.

The method usually involves collecting information, taking notes and recording sources of information, organising the information and checking that all the relevant facts have been covered.

(i) Collecting information

Reports require you to collect information from a number of places. Some information will come directly from people in the form of interviews, telephone conversations, letters or memos. Other information will come from books, leaflets, newspaper articles, technical manuals, brochures, written statements etc.

Exercise 2 (y)

Make a list of the likely sources of information in:

(a) The Wessex Mower report
(b) The Pestco Oil Service Station report

(ii) Taking notes and recording sources of information

Whenever you gather information, it is important to keep a note of where, when and from whom or what your information comes. This enables you to:

- explain your sources of information
- check one source against another
- return to a source for further information or checking

Consider these methods of recording information:

- flow charts
- spider notes or spray notes
- report cards
- ring binder or folder of A4 pages
- computer disc or data base

Which do you prefer and why?

(iii) Organising the information

The information you gather for a report needs to be organised in a way that makes the report easy to follow and understand. To do this you need to make a plan of how you will structure your report. For example:

Failure in the new 300 series model mower

Introduction – Terms of reference

Method – Examination of 60 mowers
Study of 16 service centre reports
Study of similar faults in other models
Study of 32 customers' letters of complaint

Limitations – Need for more inspections
Need for interview with retailers

Conclusion –Two major manufacturing faults identified

Recommendations – Re-design motor housing
Replace plastic control switch arm
Re-call all 300 series mowers for changes

Exercise 2 (z)

Devise a similar plan for the Pestco Oil Service Station report. You can assume the following information was established during investigation:

- the fire was caused by the careless use of a petrol nozzle in the presence of someone smoking
- eyewitness reports confirm the cause
- more instruction and warning signs are needed

(iv) Checking that all relevant facts have been covered

Once you have organised your information you need to study your material for anything important that may have been left out. To do this effectively you should use a checklist. Have you:

- made clear the terms of reference?
- produced a relevant and precise title?
- written an introduction which makes clear the background, purpose, audience and structure?
- commented on your method?
- stated the limitations?
- decided on your findings?

(f) Conclusions

Once you have studied all the evidence and information available through your research and investigation, you now have to draw up conclusions. Conclusions can be written as essay-type prose, but if there are several they are best listed and numbered.

Sometimes the conclusion is placed in the front of a report because that is the information that the reader will want to know first.

Wherever it is placed it needs to:

- refer to the purpose of the report
- state the main points arising in the report
- be brief and conclusive

For example:

Conclusion

My investigation into the cause of repeated failure of the 300 series Wessex mower leads me to the following conclusions:

(a) The cause can be traced directly to two significant manufacturing faults:

(i) First, the motor housing, which is too big for the motor, causes vibration and loosening of parts.

(*ii*) Second, the plastic control switch arm which is made of a thin, brittle material, tends to snap after repeated use.

(*b*) Complaints from service centres about bad design are justified.

(*c*) Complaints from customers about dangerous faults are justified.

I have made some clear and urgent recommendations.

Now try to write a conclusion to the Pestco Oil Service Station report. Remember to use the plan you have already devised.

(g) Recommendations

Any recommendations that are made should be clearly presented and follow logically from the conclusions. For example:

I recommend the following:

(*a*) Re-design motor housing on all 300 series models.

(*b*) Replace plastic control switch arm on same.

(*c*) Immediate re-call of all 300 series mowers for changes.

The language and presentation of reports

Reports tend to be more formal than other forms of communication. They avoid niceties of address and are generally impersonal, with no digression from the main point of the report. The language should be simple and concise. Thinking of your reader helps to establish the right tone. As a general rule it is best to be direct and matter of fact. Avoid:

- being friendly and trendy ('it's not on man')
- being too pompous or full of self-importance ('I believe this to be utter nonsense')

You should by now have a good idea of how to structure a report. Generally they follow this kind of structure in the form of paragraphs:

- title – needs to be precise and relevant
- introduction – refers to terms of reference, and background
- main body – states the method, limitations and findings
- conclusions – refers to purpose, makes main points and is conclusive and brief
- recommendations – clearly presented and logical, follow on from conclusions

Using illustrations or images in your report

You will find lots of suggestions and ideas in the *Images* chapter of this book on how and when to use images and illustrations in your report. Generally you should use an illustration or image when the information can be shown more effectively than the written word.

Remember to:

- make sure the illustration is relevant and positioned in the right place

- check that the illustration is well labelled and makes a clear point
- keep the illustration as simple as possible

As a final exercise on reports, collect as many examples of reports as you can find and consider how they have been written and produced. Look for strengths and weaknesses and features that are worth remembering.

Log books

The log book is another example of the outline format where written information appears in set places. Since the main purpose of the log book is to record, you can expect to find information such as the time, date, name and subject heading arranged in a way that is easy to complete and read.

Guests' Log Book

Date of Arrival	Time	Name	Signature	Date of Departure

Log books may be used to record many different activities, including a demanding task like keeping track of GNVQ assignments. Unlike a day page diary, where there is a limited space for each day's entries, the outline format of the log book allows you to design the layout to your individual needs and to write as much as you need for each entry.

The log book needs to be legible and accurate because it is often used as a means of checking records and information. A GNVQ student's log book, for example, may be used as a record of meeting course requirements and claiming credits. It can also be used to track progress and help decide which main subject and core skill performance criteria still need to be covered.

Consider this example where each sheet is added to a ring binder to form a student's log of assignments, criteria and range covered:

GNVQ STUDENT'S LOG

Assignment Title:

Range covered:	Performance Criteria:

Student's Comment:

Tutor's Comment:

Date Set:	When By:	Date finished:

Working on logs

Find an example of a log book in use in your school or college. Consider these points:

- is the format easy to follow, and if not why not?
- what purpose does this log book serve?
- is the log book used by more than one person, and if so, does everyone follow the headings accurately? If there is a problem, how may this be solved?

Skills in practice

An exercise on crime and punishment

The following exercise is designed for Intermediate and Advanced Level students. The assignments and written work produced relate to the skills and range of written work you have studied in the previous chapters. In this exercise you will be asked to work in a small group and produce letters and reports.

The performance criteria you can achieve in this unit are as follows.

(a) The information is accurate and suitable to the needs of the audience or those who are meant to read it.

(b) Documents are legible.

(c) Grammar, punctuation and spelling follow standard rules or conventions and words used routinely and frequently are spelt correctly.

(d) The format used is suitable to the nature of the material and information is organised to maximise audience understanding.

(e) The effectiveness of your own organisation and presentation of material is evaluated accurately for strengths and weaknesses.

The best of this material can be selected for your portfolio as evidence of core skills communications achievement.

Your first task is to read the following background information on crime and punishment.

Background information

According to Home Office statistics, over eight million working days are lost by men and women serving prison sentences in this country. At least 1,500 of these are serving life sentences for serious crimes such as murder and terrorism. The rest of the prison population is made up of those serving various terms of imprisonment for offences that range from theft and handling stolen goods to violence and sexual offences against the person.

Criminology – the study of crime and criminals – has supplied the police and those who deal directly with crime with much useful analysis, statistics and information. But there is as yet no definite reason why one person takes to crime and another does not. In seeking to understand crime, criminologists tell us it is important to look beyond the immediate causes (boredom, greed, anger) to deeper underlying causes. These deeper causes may include the following:

(a) Social pressures – the constant stream of materialistic values conveyed through advertising, television programmes, newspapers, popular fashion in dress.

(b) Conflict – with family (husband or wife) or with friends; between ethnic, religious or political groups; with authority.

(c) Mental and emotional disorders – those who suffer from serious psychological disorders, sexual maladjustment; psychopathic tendency.

(d) Personal circumstances – unemployment; poverty; lack of, or bad housing; difficult home situation.

Now consider the following crimes and read the section which follows on prisoner's rights.

MUDDLE BEHIND MILKMAN'S THEFT

A MILK roundsman's thefts of nearly £727 in cash came from 'muddled book-keeping' magistrates at Wareham were told.

John Butler (30) of West Drayton, London, admitted false accounting and stealing £726.36.

He was sentenced to120 hours of community service work for the offences.

The court heard that Butler had worked for Unigate Dairies at Wool and the offences came to light after he had been warned by the company about shortages. In a survey, 47 customers said they had paid their bills when in Butler's book it was shown they still owed cash.

Defending, Mr. Patrick Miles gave the court cash and milk coupons totalling the £145.50 compensation the dairy had asked for.

He told the court: 'The offence is born out of muddled book-keeping – not downright dishonesty.'

Butler had worked as a milk roundsman previously and then run a pub before becoming a milkman again.

PENSIONS FRAUD MAN IS GAOLED

A HIGH-LIVING executive, Robert Brundle, swindled more than £4000,000 out of his employers, the White Star Insurance Company, in a pensions fraud which went on for 15 years, Bolton Crown Court heard yesterday.

Brundle, aged 44, of Bolton, who admitted conspiracy to defraud, false accounting and three charges of theft, was sentenced to a total of three and a half years' imprisonment. A colleague, Ian Holland, 61, of Harling, Essex, who admitted a joint charge of conspiracy, was gaoled for two years.

MAN ON PAROLE RAPED GIRL, 13

GERALD MORLAND was gaoled for life yesterday for raping a 13-year-old girl while on parole from a sentence for raping two other teenage girls.

Morland, aged 40, abducted the girl from the house of a woman friend with whom he had had an argument.

The girl, who was baby-sitting, attempted to escape. Morland threatened her with scissors, pushed her into a hired car, and subjected her to a four-hour ordeal.

His attack came seven months after he was released from gaol. He had served less than two years of a four-year sentence for the rape of a 14-year-old and a 15-year-old girl.

Yesterday at Headingly Crown Court Morland admitted one offence of rape, two of attempted rape and one of abduction. He was given three life sentences to run concurrently.

Mr. Justice Varney told him: 'You are a continuing and positive menace. You are not mentally ill but suffer from a personality disorder.'

The court had heard that Morland was also gaoled for 12 months in March 1977 for indecently assaulting a five-year-old girl.

'WENT BERSERK' MAN JAILED

A 27-YEAR-OLD man 'went berserk' with an open Stanley knife in a crowded store, Fulham magistrates were told.

'He went around the store with the open knife, knocking over stands and pulling to the floor items displayed for sale', said Mrs. Carol Barber, prosecuting.

Vincent John Oakley, of no fixed address, pleaded guilty to stealing a bottle of gin valued £14.95 from Snell & Co wine store; to possessing an offensive weapon, a knife, while in that store; to causing damage to a curtain roll the property of Brooks Brothers; and again to having a knife while in that store.

The chairman of the Bench, Mr. John Ellaway, told Oakley that in view of his record and the seriousness of the offences they had very little choice but to impose a custodial sentence. He was sentenced to six months' imprisonment on each offence to run concurrently.

The prisoner's rights

Once a person has been sentenced to a term of imprisonment they have the following rights:

Books:	Although limited, library facilities are available. Reading material sent to the prison is allowed but may be censored.
Clothing:	Men must wear uniforms (women don't have to).
Discharge Grant:	A prisoner receives a small sum of money to help him or her on release.
Discipline:	Punishments include punishment cells, withdrawn privileges, loss of remission and earnings, confinement.
Food:	Three meals a day.
Letters:	Prisoners may send and receive one letter a week. The authorities read all letters except legal ones.
Parole:	After serving one third of a sentence a prisoner can be considered for parole.
Remission:	One third of a sentence can be reduced for good conduct.
Visits:	One visit per month of at least 30 minutes.
Work:	On average, 24 hours a week for small pay.
Parole:	Except in cases where a judge has stated a person should serve not less than a given number of years, or be detained indefinitely, prisoners have the right to be considered for parole. The Parole Board consists of a small number of professional individuals not directly associated with the prison service. It is the board who decide the outcome of each parole application. Because of the serious and grave consequences of a wrong decision, the Parole Board has to consider each case very carefully.

Decision making

The following four prisoners now qualify for parole. In a small group you are the Parole Board meeting to decide which one of the four prisoners is most suitable for parole. In the group discussion it is necessary for each individual to express considered opinions and show an understanding of the contributions of other group members. (See the chapters on Oral work – working in a group).

In making a decision of this nature the Parole Board would most certainly consider the points below.

(a) That the offender has served at least one third of his/her sentence.

(b) The behaviour of the prisoner while in prison.

(c) Evidence that the offender has expressed regret and a coming to terms with his/her crime.

(d) Is the offender likely to commit a crime again?

(e) Will they have somewhere to live on leaving prison?

(f) Will they have support from family or friends?

(g) What opportunities exist for future employment and social rehabilitation?

(h) Is there good evidence of emotional and personal stability?

CASE REPORT

Here are the case reports on each prisoner

Name:	Robinson, James
Age:	45 years
Offence:	Manslaughter. Assaulting a Police Officer. Nothing previous.
Date of conviction and sentence:	1.5.92 12 Years

Remarks:

James is a married man with three children, all of secondary school age. Educated at Charter House and Radley College, James obtained a first class degree from London University in History and for four years after graduating worked for a firm of brokers in London.

Prior to his conviction James was self employed as an antiques dealer in Norfolk where his offence was committed.

Since admission, James still maintains his innocence in the killing of his former business partner, who was shot with an antique pistol shortly after the two rowed violently. He says his wife is suffering terrible hardship bringing up the children on her own. James himself is suffering from repeated bouts of depression. A quiet but excitable man, James says he will emigrate to Australia if paroled.

CASE REPORT

Name: Morris, Patrick

Age: 25 Years

Offence:

Date of conviction and sentence: 6.6.91
10 Years

Remarks:

Patrick is a man of extremely limited intelligence. At the time of his offence he was working on a building site where he plunged a pickaxe into the chest of a JCB driver who nudged him into a trench during a prank. Patrick says he cannot remember much of what happened that afternoon, but that he completely lost his temper and never meant to harm the man fatally.

In prison Patrick has learnt three new skills and is much liked by fellow prisoners and prison staff alike. His mother is anxious to have him home where there is a room for him and the opportunity of a permanent job in a local bakery.

CASE REPORT

Name: Gilmore, William

Age: 23 years

Offence: Robbery with violence.
Armed robbery.
Taking and driving away a vehicle.
Conspiracy to evade arrest.

Date of conviction and sentence: 21.5.93
38 Years

Remarks: After both his parents were killed in a road traffic accident, William spent most of his childhood in the care of the Social Services. William experienced difficulties in various schools until he was fostered and attended a special school for children with emotional and behavioural problems where he settled down well.

On leaving school William worked on various farms in rural Dorset as a labourer and tractor driver. A year prior to his crime, William moved to a bedsit in London and believes it was the city life that brought him into contact with the wrong people.

William says he is at home in the countryside and dislikes cities. His great love is horses and while in prison William has performed exceptionally as a groom in the stables attached to the prison. Recently William has had the offer of a permanent job on a local dairy farm. If released William says he will settle down to a quiet country living.

CASE REPORT

Name:	Martindale, Gregory
Age:	40 years
Offence:	Infanticide Own Child. Nothing previous.
Date of conviction and sentence:	23.1.89 15 Years

Remarks:

Gregory was working as a travelling salesman at the time of his offence, which took place during a violent row with his wife. Gregory's other two children are still with his wife and the family visit him regularly. Mrs. Martindale appears to have forgiven her husband for the death of the baby and holds herself partly to blame. She says she is willing to have her husband back and believes the children need their father home.

Since admission, Gregory has attended several classes in the prison and has managed to obtain 6 GCSEs in science and arts subjects. While in prison Gregory has discovered he is gifted musically and has become expert on the guitar.

Gregory's attitude to his crime is complex. He believes his long spells away from home were partly to blame for what eventually happened. He also holds his wife's parents responsible because of their 'needling'. Gregory has been overheard to say he will 'fix' his father-in-law, but warders believe this may be bravado. Recently Gregory has received the offer of a job as rhythm guitarist with a jazz band.

Findings

In making a decision of this nature there is unlikely to be a right or wrong choice. Each case is judged on its merits and ultimately it is a question of who is the most suitable candidate.

Oral presentation

Each group is now asked to present its findings to the class, i.e. choice of prisoner for parole and reasons for this choice. To do this effectively, it is necessary to plan and prepare as a group. Here are some points to consider for your presentation:

(a) Will one, two or all members of the group contribute to the actual presentation?

(b) How will your group organise its findings and justify its conclusions?

(c) Will you invite questions from the class during your presentation?

(d) Will you use any images to enhance your presentation? (See the *Images* section on visual aids)

Written work

Having discussed and presented your findings as a group, each student now has the task of drafting a set of four written reports on each of the parole cases. You will find it useful to revise the section on *Report writing* before you begin this task. When you have completed your first draft try this checklist:

- ▶ Are the terms of reference clear?
- ▶ Has each report achieved its purpose (informed and explained)?
- ▶ Are the points made in the reports organised in a logical and orderly way?
- ▶ Are your opinions supported by evidence or sound argument?
- ▶ Do your reports avoid jargon (unintelligible or meaningless writing)?
- ▶ Does the closing paragraph in each report summarise earlier points and tie up loose ends?

You will find it a useful exercise to let a partner read over your reports using the above checklist as a guide.

Written presentation

Before producing your final draft you should use a dictionary or spell-checker for mis-spelling and other errors of presentation. Remember to make use of any presentational devices available, such as a typewriter or word processor.

Revise the chapter on letter writing before you begin the next task.

Three letters

(a) A formal letter to the successful prisoner. In the role of the chairman of the Parole Board write a letter to the successful applicant informing him of his parole. Again there is a need to be clear and precise in your organisation. The prisoner has the right to know the basis of your judgment. You can also suggest any special conditions attached to parole, e.g. report to local Police Station once a week etc.

(b) The successful prisoner's reply. Your aim here is to produce a convincing response from the prisoner. The prisoner's language is likely to be characterised by a personal style, perhaps using non-standard forms of English.

(c) A formal letter to an unsuccessful prisoner. You may find it appropriate to keep this letter brief, to the point, but also courteous and expressing some hope.

3

Using images

Illustrations and images in your writing and discussion

It is said that pictures or images speak louder than words. Look at this image. What does it make you think about?

Bucchi, Italy Source: 'Thin Black Lines', DEC, 1988

In 1985 the Band Aid/Live Aid project used this image and others to help make people aware of the drought-affected areas of Africa. The project was a tremendous success. You may remember some of the scenes shown on television and in the cinema. The images, without words, spoke for themselves.

Images with or without words can be a powerful and direct way of communicating. They can condense a large amount of information into a small space.

Why we use images

Images are used for a variety of reasons:

- images are easily understood by everyone
- images communicate ideas much quicker than words
- one image on a page is cheaper to produce than a page of words
- images have more impact because most people prefer to spend less time reading
- images are easy to remember

Of course, not everything can be communicated in images. Getting to know how, when and where to use images correctly are all important communication skills your GNVQ will help you develop. In this chapter you will :

- get to know the range or type of images you are expected to use
- get to know the range of situations in which you use images
- try some exercises using these images
- get some practice in creating and using a range of images

The range of images used in GNVQ

For all Levels, Foundation, Intermediate and Advanced, in your Core and Option unit assignments you can use any form of *readily available* image in your writing or talking.

Readily available means any image that is ready at hand and does not have to be specially produced. This can include images such as:

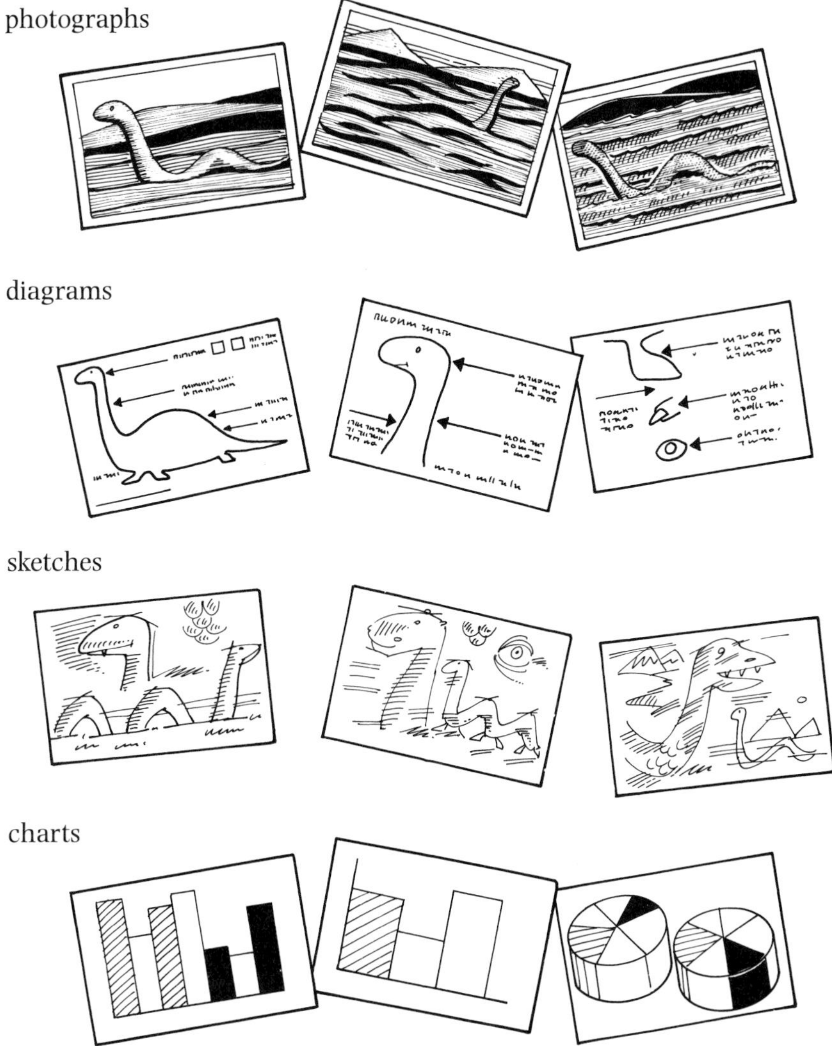

Graphs (line, polygons & histograms)

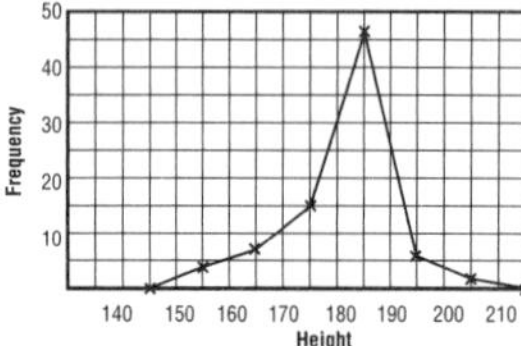
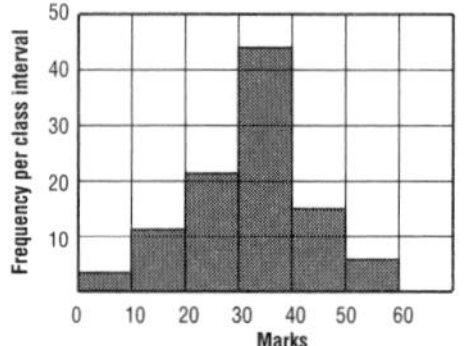
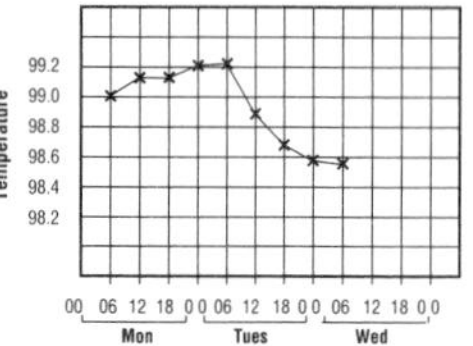

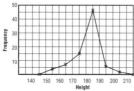

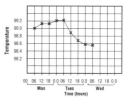

symbols

tables

Village	Number of students
Ashurst	31
Botleigh	15
Crow	28
Downton	24
Eaglecliffe	19
Fillingdales	33
Total	**150**

Village	Number of students	
	Male	Female
Ashurst	15	16
Botleigh	10	5
Crow	13	15
Downton	12	12
Eaglecliffe	11	8
Fillingdales	13	20
Total	**74**	**76**

Speed of cars (mph)	Frequency
0–39	0
40–49	7
50–59	54
60–69	75
70–79	25
80–89	2

Above Foundation Level there are some extra requirements:

For Intermediate and Advanced Levels you are **also** expected to use images which have been specially produced to suit your subject. This refers to images like still photographs, drawings, graphs and sketches that are specially organised or created by you for a particular purpose.

No. of sightings of the Loch Ness Monster
As you can see, these statistics present an interesting picture.

The quality of the illustrations and images you use is called (the *performance criteria)*

- For all Levels, Foundation, Intermediate and Advanced, the illustrations and images you use need to be:
  - relevant or related to the main points you are making
  - designed to make your subject easy to follow
  - used in the right place at the right time
- For Advanced Level, the illustrations and images you use need to be:
  - relevant or related to your main points and other points which your audience may find difficult to follow
  - designed to make your subject easy to follow
  - used in the right place at the right time

  and you need to be able to:
  - evaluate the effectiveness of your own and others' use of images

Looking at images

Exercise 3 (a) E

Look at the photograph and diagram below. Both represent the same thing. Yet each one gives a different impression. What qualities do you think each image has for use in an assignment?

If you were producing an assignment on cars, when would be the right time and place to use:

(a) the photograph *(b)* the diagram

Explain what effect you would hope to achieve with each. What other images might you use in this assignment?

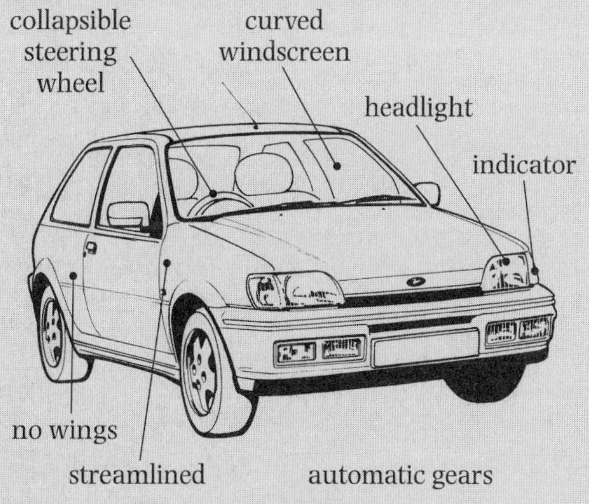

Look at these ways of presenting information using images. Some, like the pie chart, are easy to read and tell you information quickly. Others, like the detailed map and bar chart, need to be studied more carefully.

Diagrams, which are often used in manufacturing industry, tell you about the pieces or components of an object and how it works. Labelled diagrams are often used in technical reports. You will find out more about using charts and graphs in your Application of Number core skills.

Maps

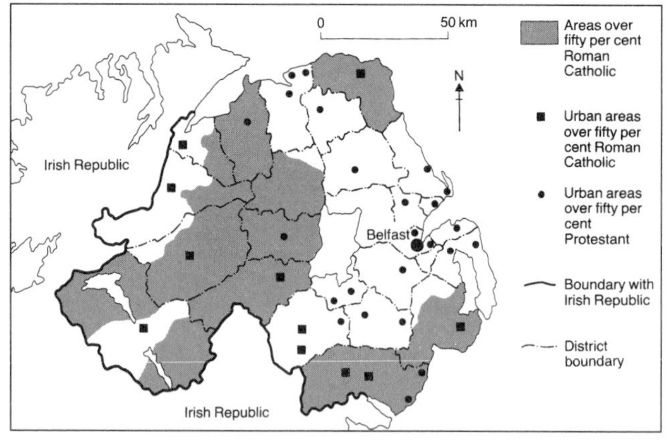

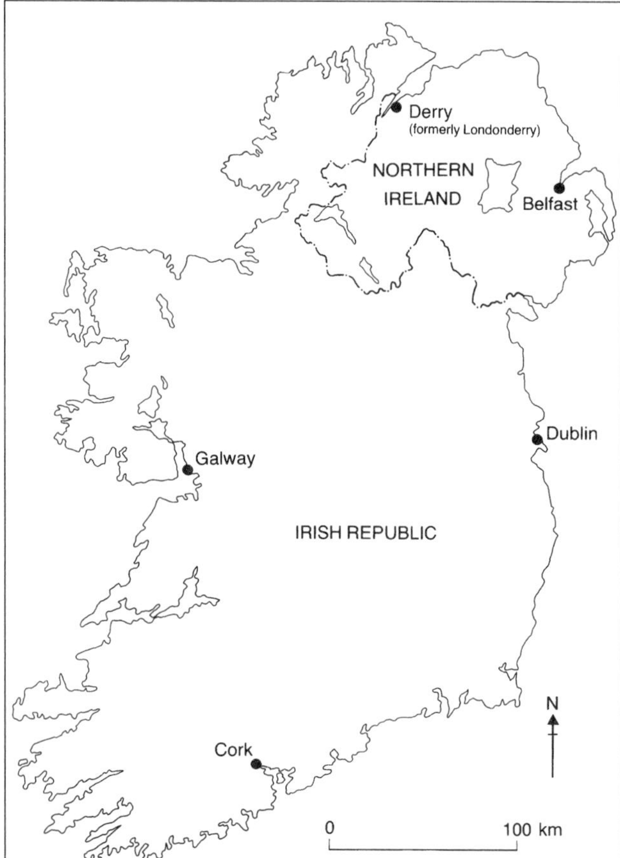

Diagrams

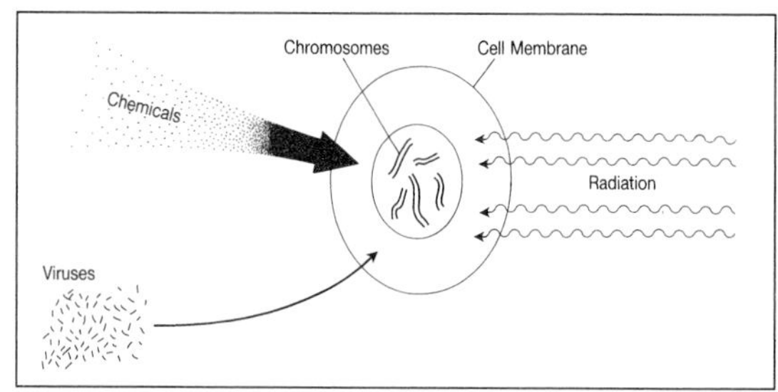

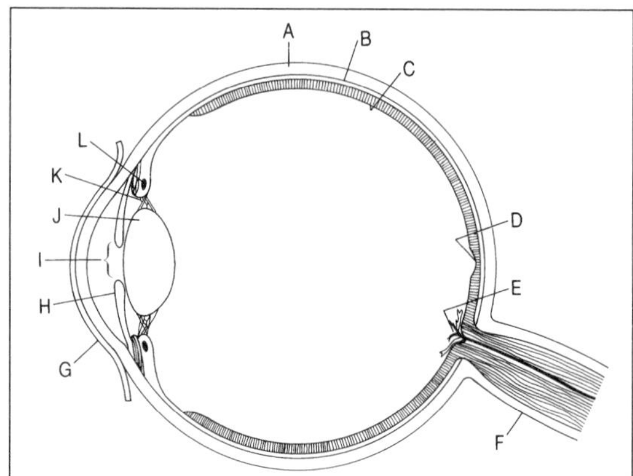

Graph

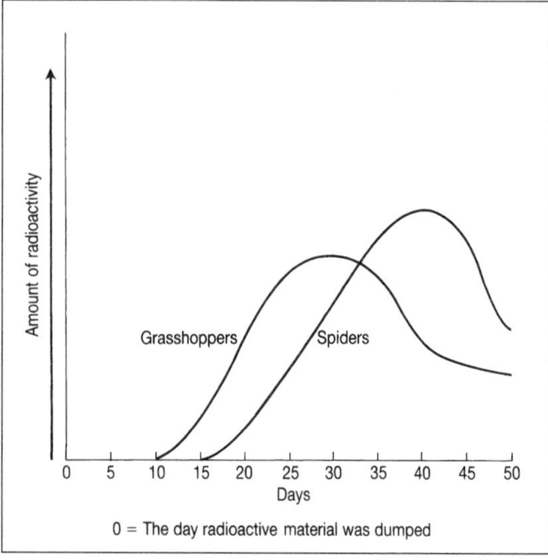

Bar chart

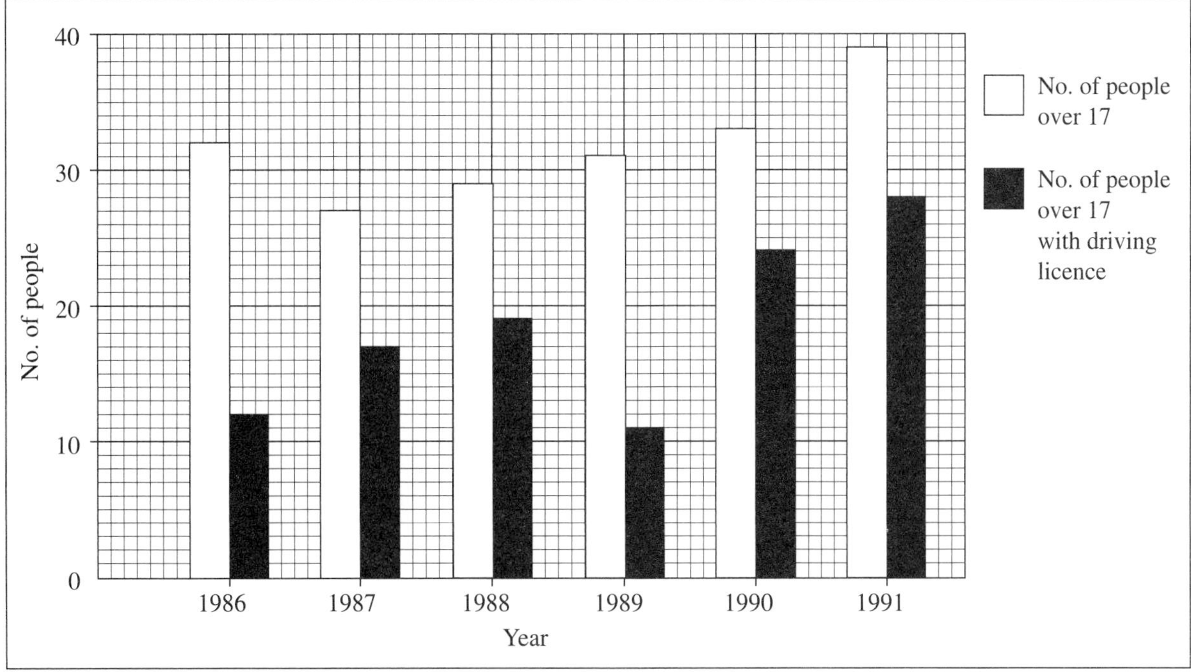

Pie chart

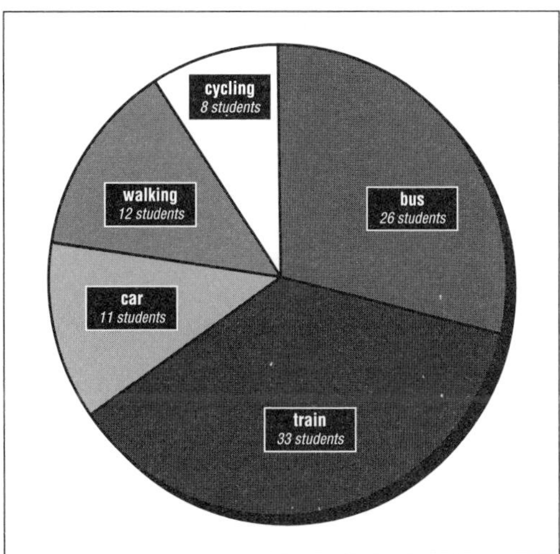

Exercise 3 (b)

E

What kind of images do you think would be useful for the following assignments?

(a) A written assignment on student travel to and from college.

(b) A talk to a group of fellow students on the dangers of smoking.

(c) A talk to a small group of Year 11 secondary students on what your school or college has to offer students who wish to study GNVQ.

(d) A written project on how to improve the local environment.

When and where to use images

Here are some basic tips:

- Use an image *only* if it makes the point better than words or talk.
- Always put yourself in the position of the reader or listener and ask yourself – Is this the best way of communicating my point or information?
- Your images should be clear and, if included in a written assignment, well placed near to the point mentioned (or perhaps it would be better as an appendix?)
- The image should speak for itself, but you may have to introduce it or explain its relevance.
- Keep your images as simple as possible, without trying to convey too much information in one image.
- Always use a title, heading or caption above or below your image so that the audience can tell at a glance what it shows.
- In the case of a written assignment, keep your image to a sensible scale so that it can be understood easily.
- Always consider assignments in the planning stage and ask yourself – Is there scope here for an image or illustration? If so, then what kind? Remember all of the above points.

Images in written work

In a written assignment it is possible to have a range of images to help communicate your ideas. Suppose you were producing a written assignment on cameras. Apart from words, you could have:

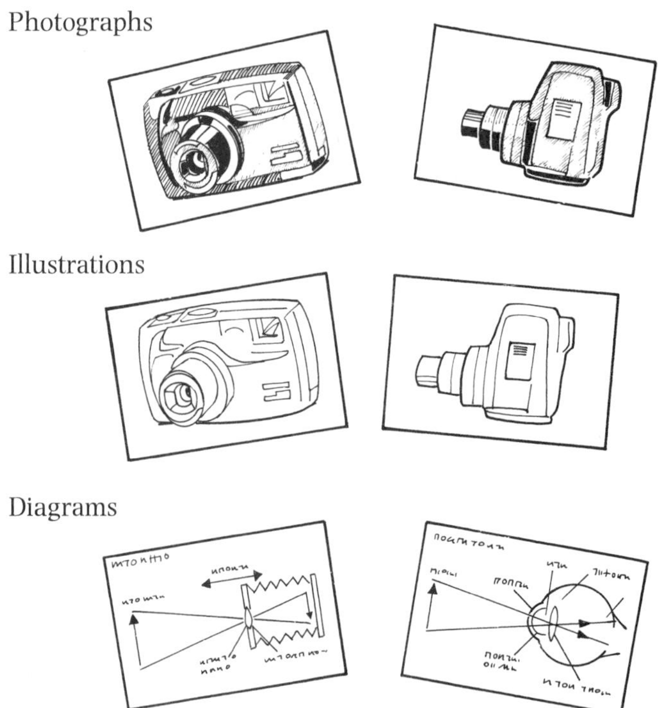

Snap shots

The written work along with some of the images could also be produced on computer.

Images in discussion and oral presentations

Using images in a discussion or oral presentation requires the use of different visual aids. For example:

- large posters or flip charts
- video and TV screen to show moving images
- chalkboard or whiteboard for any form of chart, diagram or illustration
- OHP (overhead projector) for images prepared in advance like maps, detailed diagrams etc. The information can be slowly revealed in sequence.
- slides for still images which can be enlarged for general classroom viewing. Readily available slides are easy to get for most subjects, and it is possible to produce your own slides without too much extra expense.
- photocopied images or illustrations provide your audience with permanent reference material during your talk.
- computers (particularly those with a CD-ROM drive) can provide high quality still or moving images to support a talk or discussion.

Remember: before you use an image you have to decide why you are using it and what purpose it will serve.

Will it:

- Display information or offer a quick summary?
- Show some kind of comparison (e.g. bar or line graph, pie chart)?
- Show details about a machine, object or process (e.g. diagram or flow chart)?
- Create an impression or cause an emotional reaction (e.g. photograph – black and white or full colour?)?
- Serve as an introduction, summary or end to an assignment (e.g. photograph, chart or diagram)?
- Introduce new/old information in a better way?
- Show how something works (diagram, sketch, photograph)?

Here are some exercises on how, when and where to use images in your discussion and written work.

E

Exercise 3 (c)

Read the following three situations and then decide which images from the list could have been used by each of the students. Not all of the images are suitable to the tasks.

Situation A

Alan's task is to give a talk to his class in which he will explain what changes he would make to his college environment in order to accommodate more physically disabled students, such as the blind, deaf and those in wheelchairs.

Situation B

As part of her business studies, Rukshana's task is to produce a written assignment in which she describes how she developed a mini enterprise scheme, producing, advertising and selling friendship bracelets.

Situation C

Elizabeth's task is to give an oral presentation in which she explains how she worked with a group of four other students to produce a health and safety guide for students using the science labs in her college.

Images which may have been used by any of the above students in their tasks are:

- fire hazard symbol
- bar graph showing numbers and types of disability among college students
- photograph of main door and college car park
- photograph of students using hand tools to produce bracelets
- do not exceed 30 mph speed limit sign
- pie chart showing range and types of accidents experienced in schools and colleges
- photograph of college sports centre
- outline plan of college building, including stairways, fire escapes, toilets and main entrance
- diagrams showing how to give first aid
- plan of science lab with arrows pointing to potential hazards
- symbol for wheelchair
- slippery surface sign
- symbol for poison
- go slow sign
- photograph of students at a party

Using images in your writing and discussion will improve your communication and help others to understand your subject.

The situation

This section looks at the range of situations for which you should use images.

At all levels, Foundation, Intermediate and Advanced, you should use images in your Core and Option unit assignments when:

- the subject you are talking or writing about is your day-to-day work. *For example* – Talking to a group of fellow students about your ideas on how to get to a place using a map or atlas is appropriate.

  Or, in a written assignment you want to explain the distribution of tropical rain forests in the world; using graphs and pie charts from a geography text book will be useful here.
- you know the people you are writing or talking for and they know about the subject. *For example* – friends, colleagues, relatives, fellow students, supervisors, teachers and tutors.

When you produce a GNVQ assignment, who reads it? What influence, if any, does this have on the images you use?

Exercise 3 (d)

E

Here is an example of a situation in which a student uses images in an assignment.

(a) Caroline was asked to present ideas to her college class on how she would improve the college sports centre. Caroline thought it would be a good idea to borrow plans and photographs from the sports office to use in her presentation. This is what she was able to borrow:

- a large A3 size colour photograph of the main sports hall
- a printed plan of the main sports facilities, e.g. sauna, squash courts, swimming pool, changing rooms etc.
- an outline sketch of the tennis courts

Imagine you were in the class when Caroline gave her three minute presentation. Caroline had ideas on making the sports hall bigger, building an extra two changing rooms and adding an extra two tennis courts. Give a brief oral or written account of her presentation. Explain how she used her images and illustrations.

or

(b) Apart from the photograph, create the second two images that Caroline used.

You use images and illustrations at Intermediate Level when:

- the subject you are talking or writing about is your day-to-day work. *For example* - day-to-day organisation and administration, such as replying to customers' letters or explaining to a group of fellow students your ideas on how to set up a science experiment.

- you don't know the people you are writing or talking to, but they know about the subject.
  For example – those with whom you are not in frequent contact, e.g. customers and clients in a business organisation.

Exercise 3 (d)

Michelle has received a letter from her local council concerning a proposed route for a new communications cable that is about to be laid under the footpath in front of her house. Michelle objects to this route because she believes the digging and cable run will result in an uneven footpath surface.

Michelle decides to write to the council with a detailed plan of where she thinks the cable should be laid.

Imagine you are Michelle, write her letter of objection and devise her alternative detailed plan.

You use images and illustrations at Advanced Level when:

- the subject you are talking or writing about is not only your day-to-day work, but also on subjects which are non-routine and sometimes complicated.
  For example – handling customers' letters, reporting on a piece of research, writing about or discussing a sensitive issue.
- you don't know the people and they don't know the subject.
  For example – customers, clients, visitors who have no prior knowledge of the subject and need careful and detailed explanations.

Exercise 3 (e)

Ved works part time on reception in a small local hotel. The manager of the hotel asks Ved to devise a simple and easy to follow plan of the hotel as an aid to all receptionists when explaining the hotel's plan to guests. The hotel is a two storey building with fourteen bedrooms, two large reception rooms, a bar, main dining room and kitchen.

The manager wanted the plan to fit on one side of A4 paper.

Draw the plan as Ved might have done. Include room numbers and all other important information you feel receptionists and guests would need.

Pie charts, bar charts and histograms

Pie charts

Pie charts are often a good way of presenting numerical facts.

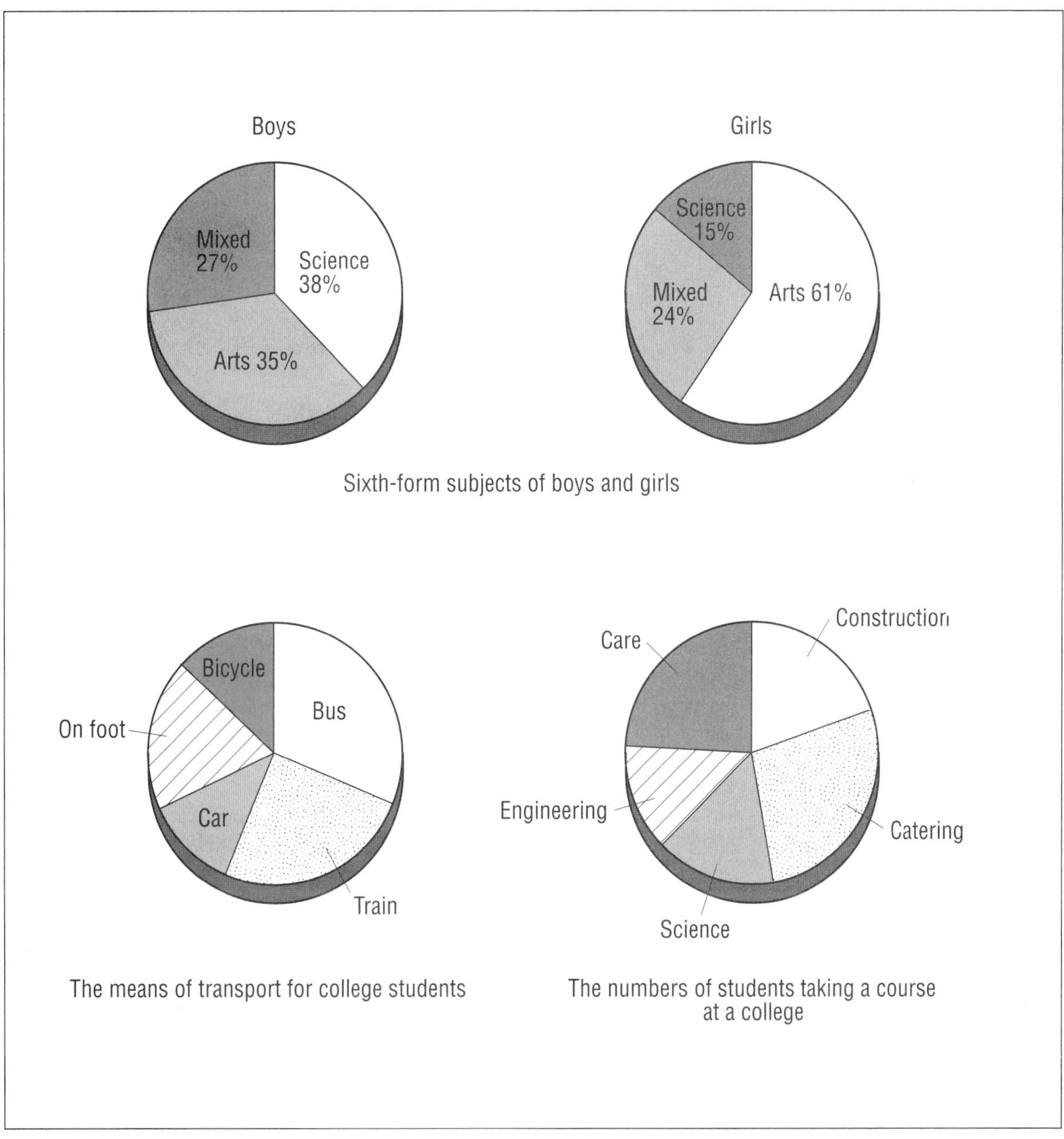

What information and impressions do these pie charts tell at a glance? In what type of assignment are you likely to find these charts? What background information do you think was needed to produce these charts and how do you think the information was gathered?

You will find more information and instructions on how to produce pie charts in your Application of Number core skills.

Exercise 3 (f)

Create a pie chart to show the following information about books sold in a town bookshop during a weekend

(a) Sport and hobbies 25%
(b) Computer 15%
(c) Biography 30%
(d) Fiction 20%
(e) Others 10%

Bar charts

Bar charts are another way of presenting facts. They are very useful for showing trends and comparisons.

For example:

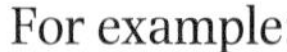

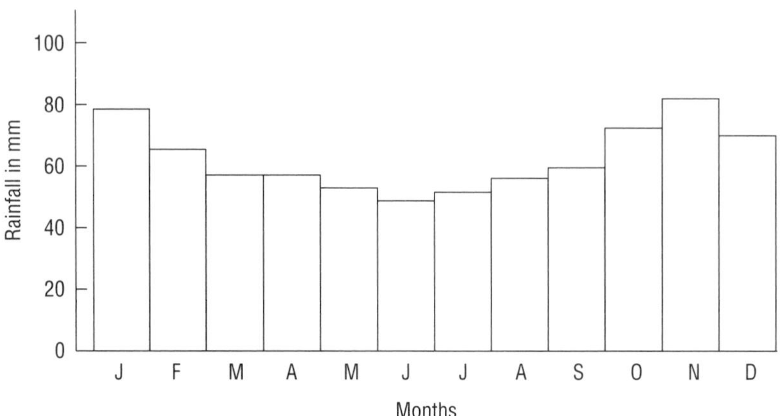

Computers are one way of producing high quality, professional images like bar and pie charts, graphs and even illustrations.

Histograms

The histogram is a series of bar charts placed beside each other for comparison. The audience or reader can see a trend for each category over a period of time. The three-dimensional effect is easily obtained with computer graphics.

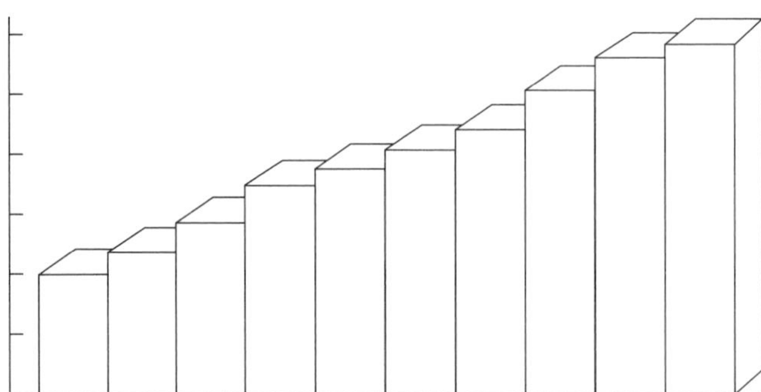

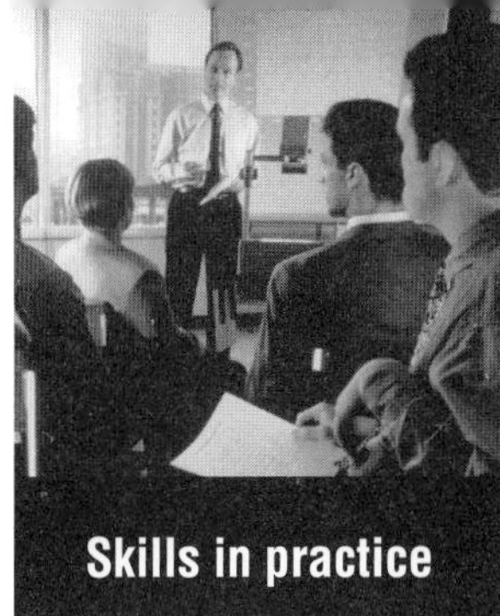

Skills in practice

Exercises in the use of images in writing and discussion

Exercise 3 (g)

E

List the type of images you would to expect to find in the following:

- A police report on a road traffic accident
- A car manual
- A school's GCSE examination results
- A handbook for a personal computer
- A book on flower arranging
- A science text book
- A book on business skills
- An information leaflet for a sports centre
- A media studies text book
- A tourist information leaflet
- Guitar For Beginners book

Exercise 3 (h)

E

Conduct a survey in your class on student means of transport to and from college or school. Present the information collected in the following forms:

(a) A bar chart *(b)* A pie chart *(c)* A histogram

Exercise 3 (i)

E

Your tutor has asked you and three other students to produce an information booklet. The booklet should have four A4 pages and the purpose is to introduce new students to GNVQ. Apart from text, you have been asked to include a mixture of images. What images would you consider relevant in this assignment? Make a list.

Exercise 3 (j)

E

Madhur has just completed a long written assignment on her part in a Young Enterprise scheme. The scheme involved producing a recipe book containing fifty recipes of popular and cheap meals for students.

Madhur's job was to select the best and most popular recipes from the many hundreds her team received from students. Madhur also had to produce a front cover for the book using a number of drawings from her team on the theme of student food. Madhur's assignment covers all aspects of producing the product, as well as notes about working as a team within a period of six weeks.

Madhur has decided to include six images – a mixture of photographs, drawings and charts. List the images you think Madhur may have included. Remember to mention at what stage or part of the assignment she should use each image.

Exercise 3 (k)

Create or gather the following images:

(a) A detailed cross section of a piece of equipment you use everyday
(b) A photograph that represents your main subject
(c) A pie chart which illustrates this data:

In a theatre, the ages of 100 people were recorded as follows:

Under 20 years	30
20 to 29 years	15
30 to 39 years	12
40 to 59 years	14
60 years and over	29

(d) A detailed map of your school or college

Exercise 3 (l)

A case study in images

(Intermediate and Advanced Levels)

Jim is the secretary to a manager in the claims section of a busy insurance office. Jim's boss has been invited to present a summary of his year's correspondence and dealings to the planning and development committee of the company. The boss has decided to present her subject using a range of images and prepared text which she has given to Jim for typing. The boss has asked Jim to prepare a set of images to go with the talk.

Here is a transcript of the talk:

> This year has seen a large increase in the number of motor claims processed by our department. In fact, from a figure of just over fifty thousand claims last year, we have increased to processing eighty thousand this year. To meet this extra workload, we have employed two additional correspondents and one clerk. We have also employed two part-time copy typists.
>
> We imagine the extra business our company enjoyed following the collapse of our biggest rival was the main reason for the increased workload.
>
> The department's staff appraisal got off to a successful start and all but two junior staff have yet to be appraised. As you may know, we have followed the company's directive on appraisal and used our four middle and two senior managers to appraise our twelve correspondents, four clerks and six typists. The middle managers were themselves appraised by the senior managers who in turn were appraised by an outside manager – in our case Jackie Wright from personnel.
>
> The appraisal process has resulted in four staff registering on courses and one senior correspondent requesting early retirement.

This year has also seen the introduction of the Seeker computer network system, with a work station on every desk and laser printer for each section. All staff have now been trained on this system and we have experienced few problems, except for the loss of twenty files when the system went down during the electrical fire last October. To avoid this happening in the future, I have installed a rolling EM reminding all users to save as they work.

We look forward to a successful and no doubt busy new year.

Task

Create Jim's set of images to accompany his boss's talk. Remember all the points in the section on when and where to use images.

4

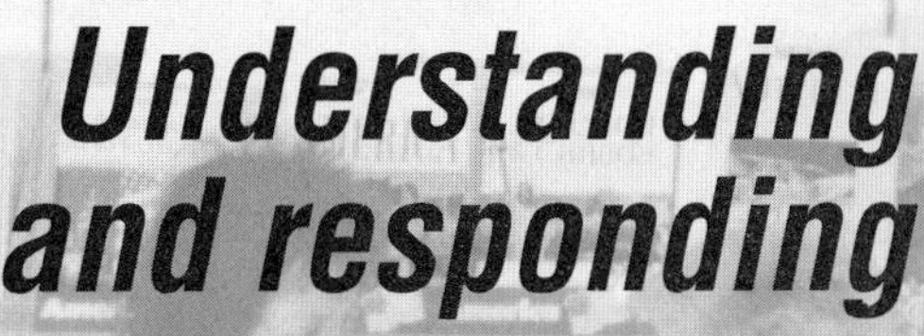

Understanding and responding

Understanding and responding to written materials and supporting illustrations

Can you tell fact from fiction?

When a Sunday newspaper printed a headline to reveal that a London bus had been discovered on the surface of the moon, most people felt they knew the story was invented. Other stories are more difficult to dismiss so easily. Some are hard to believe and hard not to believe at the same time.

What do you think of this?

> In 1989 a London University student researching the trading methods of the East Indian Tea company, made a remarkable discovery. As part of his research the student was reading the log book from the Tea Company's leading flag ship, the *Orlando*. The captain's daily entries, all written in neat italic quill, revealed the normal day-to-day business on board this large wooden cargo ship as it sailed slowly and steadily back to England with a cargo of tea.
>
> Apart from a sailor with a septic toe, the journey was uneventful and nothing unusual happened. Then at around 2.00pm on the 11th of August 1900, the captain's log revealed the details of an extraordinary event. According to the log, the ship was nearing the south coast of Madagascar when an enormous black metallic disc, twice the size of the ship, descended from the sky. The captain records a full description of the disc which he described as solid with 'no windows, doors or slots of any kind' and with a smooth metallic surface 'like the gun metal of cannon shot.'
>
> It appears the disc floated not on the surface of the waves, but three feet above it, hovering in this position for two hours. The captain notes how the disc made no noise whatsoever and 'quizzed the crew' with its mysterious silent method of propulsion. At one point the bosun reached out with a landing pole and tapped on the edge of disc, which he could just reach from the forward rigging. The bosun's tapping got no response, except a 'solid thump, like striking stone'.
>
> Suddenly, at about 4.00 pm, the mysterious disc began to loosen its control and dip into the waves. For five minutes one half lay submerged, the other raised in the air. Then without a single bubble or disturbance, the entire disc slipped below the surface and out of sight. The captain of the *Orlando* noted the exact location on the map.

Points to think about

- Is there anything about this story that makes it believable?
- If not, then what makes it unbelievable?
- If the story is false, then who made it up - the student, the captain of the *Orlando* or the journalist who reported it in the press?

There is no easy answer to these questions, because the truth is hidden from us. Perhaps the disc is somewhere off the coast of Madagascar at the bottom of the Indian Ocean, quietly swaying in the long seaweed?

Understanding how we respond to language and images is part of your study for GNVQ.

In this chapter you will get to know about:

- the range of materials you are expected to understand and respond to
- how to set about finding the meaning of unfamiliar words and images
- how to pick out the main points in source material

The range of material you are expected to respond to and understand

For all levels, Foundation, Intermediate and Advanced, you are expected to be able to understand and respond to material:

- in given formats such as signs, notices, advertisements forms, worksheets, report cards, memos
- such as simple illustrations and sketches, diagrams, photographs and charts
- presented in speech and writing about day-today familiar subjects

For Advanced Level you are **also** expected:

- to understand and respond to more complicated and difficult forms of writing and images on subjects that are more complex
- to use your own sources to discover meanings and information

The quality of your understanding and response

For all levels, Foundation, Intermediate and Advanced, you need to be able to:

- pick out the main points in material
- find out the meanings of words and images using sources provided for you

For Advanced Level you are **also** expected to:

- research and discover for yourself the sources that will help you to understand and respond to written materials and supporting illustrations

The uses of language

Language has several uses. Among them are these more common ones:

(a) to instruct – car manual, service book, text book, instruction leaflet

(b) to amuse – joke book, stories, drama script, funny story in newspaper

(c) to persuade – adverts, holiday brochure, religious leaflet

(d) to inform – newspaper, magazine, notice board

(e) to compare – student essay, report on products (*Which* magazine)

(f) to discuss – assignment, magazine article, journal

(g) to reveal – newspaper article, biography, diary, note book

Whenever we use language it is always with some use or purpose in mind. Sometimes it is obvious what we are trying to do with language.

For example:

Get Free Now's the time to go to Canada. To see your friends, or your Canadian family. It's also a good time to start planning a Canadian holiday in 1974. Air Canada has just produced a beautiful, new, *free* colour brochure full of facts and photographs and a whole host of exciting package tours. Why not send for it, read it, discuss it with your travel agent, and then come on over?
Name
Address
AIR CANADA
DTMI To: Air Canada, Dept. A, 39 Dover Street, London W1X 4ER

This newspaper advertisement makes no bones about what it is trying to sell. The language the writer uses is friendly and full of invitation, trying to convince us that 'Now's the time to go to Canada.' This is the language of invitation or persuasion.

- ▶ How does it attract your attention?
- ▶ Is the drawing important?
- ▶ What do you think of the language used?

At other times it is not so obvious what the language is trying to do. The purpose can even be hidden, as in some forms of modern advertising where the language doesn't appear to make sense until you discover it was deliberate nonsense to keep you talking and thinking about the product.

Language is like a multi -purpose tool that can do many jobs.

Look at the various uses of language again. Now match them up with these forms of writing. Some may have more than one purpose.

- A leisure centre brochure
- A safety leaflet on first aid
- A story called *The Funny Accident*
- A book called *Great Railway Journeys*
- A ghost story
- Letters from a war correspondent
- Biography of a rock star

Apart from the uses, there are three broad forms of language; functional, personal and imaginative. These are explained in the following sections.

Functional language

This is the language we use:

- to communicate information and ideas
- in the work place
- for reports and business letters
- for assignments and projects

You can recognise functional language because it:

- is without too much description
- is organised and to the point
- usually tells of facts

Exercise 4 (a)

E

Name four examples of *functional language* you use in the normal course of a week.

Personal language

This is the language we use:

- in letters to friends and family
- when we are writing about ourselves
- to give our view of an event, person or thing
  in accounts of personal experiences
- in diaries, log books and journals

You can recognise personal language because it:

- contains a personal point of view
- is full of opinions
- relates first hand experience

Exercise 4 (b)

Describe a piece of *personal language* you have produced this term.

Imaginative language

This is the language we use:

- to tell stories in speech and writing
- to be adventurous with words and meanings
- for characters and situations we imagine and invent

You can recognise imaginative language because it:

- often contains detailed, colourful descriptions
- wonders off the point to explore new meanings
- is sometimes called creative writing

Exercise 4 (c)

What do you consider to be the benefit of *imaginative language* after full-time education?

Exercise 4 (d)

(a) Look at your old school reports. How would you classify the language used in the reports?

(b) What form of language do you use mostly for your GNVQ assignments?

Using the library

Exercise 4 (e)

Visit your local school, college or town library. Discover how the system of borrowing books works, and also how to use the range of reference material available. When you have all this information arrange it into easy-to-follow steps in a flow chart. This can then be used to explain to people how the library works.

You may want to use a large piece of A3 paper to produce your flow chart. Alternatively, you could produce it on the computer. Here are some questions and situations to get you started.

- Do you want to borrow a book?
- Do you want a video or cassette tape?
- Do you want tapes or records?
- Do you only want to use the reference section?
- Do you want to browse through the books?
- Do you wish to go to the issue desk?
- Look on the newspaper rack
- Is there an author you want?

Your flow chart should cover as many alternative situations for the user as possible.

Exercise 4 (f)

E

While you are working on a long assignment, you discover you need to solve the following problems relating to understanding and response. How would you solve them?

(a) You have come across three long technical words and you have no idea what they mean.

(b) You need to find a suitable image of a motorbike to use in your assignment.

(c) You need to get all the latest information on safety clothes for motor cyclists.

Exercise 4 (g)

E

Describe in detail how you use:

(a) a dictionary

(b) an encyclopaedia

(c) the library micro film catalogue system

(d) the library index system

(e) the library subject catalogue

Selecting and rejecting points

Sometimes it is necessary to select the main points from a piece of writing.

How you decide what the important and unimportant points are depends on the material you are working with.

Consider this:

Alex won a teddy bear and a cassette tape in the college raffle

Suppose you were asked to select the main point from this statement and express it in less than five words.

You may say:

Alex won a teddy bear (you think the tape is unimportant?)

or

Alex won a cassette tape (you don't like teddy bears?)

Both of these summaries are incorrect. There is nothing in the original statement to say that the winning of the teddy bear is any more or less important than the winning of the cassette tape. You cannot reject one point at the expense of the other. So what do you do?

You have to generalise:

Alex won two prizes

Now you no longer have the full details of what Alex won, but you do have the main point.

When you are selecting points then something has to be sacrificed.

We will return to Alex in a moment. First:

A note on generalisation

Generalising, as the name suggests, refers to giving a general name to one or more items. For example:

cabbages, carrots, potatoes, cauliflowers = food

All of these are cooked and eaten. *Food* is the generalisation of them all.

It is possible to narrow the meaning a little further. Do cabbages, carrots, potatoes and cauliflower have anything else in common? – Yes, they are all vegetables. So *vegetables* is the best generalisation we have for this food.

E

Exercise 4 (h)

Try reducing these items to one generalisation:

a) London, Paris, Manchester, Bombay, Nairobi.
b) Tie, shirt, trousers, dress, blouse, pullover.
c) Cars, buses, trains, aircraft, hovercraft.
d) Football, cricket, basketball, snooker, darts.
e) Eagles, pigeons, gulls, owls.
f) Dogs, cats, camels, donkeys, snakes.
g) Knives, forks, spoons, corkscrew, pots, pans, food mixers.

Now back to Alex.

When he was a student, Alex won a teddy bear and a cassette tape of rock music in a college raffle. It was the tape that first aroused his interest in Heavy Metal and made him a famous rock guitarist. Today he is one of the foremost rock guitarists in the world.

Now, what is the most important point in the passage? Clearly the fact that Alex has become a leading rock guitarist. What about the cassette tape he won in college? This now becomes an important point in the context of the passage.

What about the teddy bear? In the context of this extended passage it is unimportant. If you were asked to pick out the main points in this new passage you would not have to generalise. You could reject the fact that Alex won a teddy bear as unimportant.

As a student Alex won a cassette tape of rock music. It was this tape that first aroused his interest in rock music and set him on the road to fame.

So before you decide what is a main point or a minor or unimportant one, you must first consider the whole passage.

Exercise 4 (i)

What do you consider to be the three main points in this passage?

It is easy to recognise a Sikh man. His wife and daughters may appear the same as other women from India, but the man himself has a special appearance. The two things which are most obvious are his turban and his beard. His turban sits low over his ears and then sweeps up each side of his forehead to form an upside-down V. Under the turban he will have long hair drawn upwards and tied in a neat knot on the top of his head. This is because Sikhs are not permitted to cut their hair.

This refusal to cut their hair also explains their beards. A Sikh's beard may be long and bushy or it may be tightly rolled. If he is a devout Sikh it will never be touched by scissors or a razor. One thing you will notice worn by a devout Sikh is a steel bangle.

Although Sikh women do not wear turbans they observe the same rules concerning uncut hair and the steel bangle. They do so because these are two of the rules laid down for all Sikhs by the tenth and last of the great teachers of the Sikh religion. Sikhs are followers of the ten Gurus. The word Guru means Master or Great Teacher, and Sikhs believe that religious truth is to be found in the teachings of their ten Masters. The first Guru was born in India more than five hundred years ago. As each died he was succeeded by another until the tenth Guru died almost three hundred years ago.

Skills in practice

E Exercise 4 (j)

What are the three main points made in this memo?

MEMORANDUM

To: Mr. C Richards. Head of Student Welfare

From: Sheila Alberta, Principal

Date: 24.3.95

Subject: Parking of bicycles

In view of the number of complaints I have received regarding parking of bicycles in and around the college grounds and buildings, I now wish the following rules to be introduced:

(a) There is to be no parking of bicycles in corridors, hallways or main driveways, or indeed in class rooms.

(b) All bicycles, including those belonging to staff, should be parked along the back wall of the canteen where parking bars already exist for over 300 bicycles. More bars will be provided if necessary.

(c) We realise there is a problem with bicycle theft and anyone who parks a bike on the college premises must secure it against theft. I have ordered extra 'lock your bike signs' from the local Police.

(d) If any bike is found outside the parking zone, it will be taken by our grounds staff and the owner will have to pay £10 for its return.

Please inform all students.

S. Alberta

Principal

Exercise 4 (k)

E

A customer's letter

You work in the box office of a busy theatre. Following a successful week's run of the Rocky Horror Show, the manager of the theatre received this letter. The manager, who is extremely busy, has asked you to identify the main points in the letter. He wants to know what has happened and what action, if any, he needs to take.

25 Princess Road
Blandford
Dorset
BH12 1BF

12 September 1995

Dear Sir/Madam

I am writing to complain about a disturbing incident I experienced in your theatre last Wednesday evening.

My family and I had just had our weekly session in the leisure pool, and we were having tea and cakes in the foyer restaurant. Suddenly a group of about a dozen young men and women swept through the restaurant squirting water pistols, waving lighters and throwing rice (yes, rice grains) over the tables and customers, including us.

I have to say I was astonished and have never experienced this type of behaviour in the leisure centre in the ten years I have been using it. What made matters worse was the ridiculous costume these yobs had dressed themselves in. The young men were wearing what appeared to be ladies' undergarments. The young women were similarly dressed in a way which can be summed up in one word – embarrassing.

Of course I realise how young people dress and how they behave should be no concern of yours, but it appears that all this was inspired by a horror play showing in your theatre.

On this matter I have only this to say – you should be more careful about the shows you present in your theatre. I believe this particular show should be banned.

I would be interested to know if you are aware of the yobbish behaviour inspired by a show performed in your theatre.

Yours disappointingly

Robert Gilmore

Index